DISCIPLINED
BY
GRACE

Other Books by J. F. Strombeck

DISCIPLINED BY GRACE

FIRST THE RAPTURE

GRACE AND TRUTH

SHALL NEVER PERISH

SO GREAT SALVATION

J. F. Strombeck

DISCIPLINED
BY
GRACE

Studies in Christian Conduct

KREGEL PUBLICATIONS
Grand Rapids, Michigan 49501

Disciplined by Grace, by J. F. Strombeck. © 1991 by Kregel Publications, a division of Kregel, Inc., P.O. Box 2607, Grand Rapids,
MI 49501. All rights reserved.

Cover Design: Don Ellens

Library of Congress Cataloging-in-Publication Data

Strombeck, J. F. (John Frederick), 1881-1959.
  Disciplined by grace / by J. F. Strombeck.
      p.   cm.
  Reprint. Originally published: Moline, IL: Strombeck Agency,
1936.

  1. Christian life. 2. Grace (Theology) I. Title.

BV4501.S7957   1991   248.4—dc20   90-22165
                                                    CIP

ISBN 0-8254-3776-8 (paperback)

            1 2 3 4 5 Printing/Year 95 94 93 92 91

            Printed in the United States of America

Contents

Foreword

When I was a very young believer, someone introduced me to the books written by J.F. Strombeck, and I bless the day it happened. *Shall Never Perish* settled for me the matter of my security in Christ, and *Grace and Truth* helped me understand the true relationship between law and grace. *Disciplined by Grace* balanced these doctrines for me and delivered me from the extremes some people go to when they first discover grace and assurance. I owe a debt of gratitude to Mr. Strombeck, and I gladly acknowledge it.

John Frederick Strombeck was born in Moline, Illinois, on December 16, 1881, into a pioneer Swedish family. Converted to Christ early in life, J.F. always sought God's leading in his decisions, both personal and business.

He started his own freight auditing business, which he managed for about ten years. When he was 25, he returned to school, first at Northwestern Academy, and then Northwestern University, from which he graduated Phi Beta Kappa in 1911. After his graduation, the Strombeck-Becker Manufacturing Company was born, specializing in various wood products. That same year he married.

J.F.'s first love was ministry in the church and with various Christian organizations that he supported. He served as a director or advisor to the Belgian Gospel Mission, Dallas Theological Seminary, Moody Bible Institute, Young Life, Inter-Varsity, and many others. While a member of the Evangelical Free Church, he was often invited to minister in the Word in various conferences, and he wrote many articles for Christian publications. The burden of foreign missions lay heavy on his heart, and he was a generous supporter of missionaries and schools that trained missionaries.

You will discover as you read each of his books that J.F. Strombeck, though a layman, had a thorough grasp of Bible doctrine and was able to apply it practically. He did not write books in order to impress, but to express what God taught him, so that you might enjoy the full blessings of salvation in Christ. I suggest that you keep your Bible close at hand as you read Strombeck's books, because he uses the Word from beginning to end!

Though J.F. Strombeck died on May 9, 1959, the investments he made in many evangelical ministries continue to produce spiritual dividends, and his Christ-centered books continue to challenge and instruct serious students of the Word. I rejoice that Kregel Publications is making these helpful volumes available to a new generation of believers.

WARREN W. WIERSBE

1

Grace Teaching Us

"F OR the grace of God that bringeth salvation hath appeared to all men, teaching us that, denying ungodliness and worldly lusts, we should live soberly, righteously, and godly, in this present world: Looking for that blessed hope, and the glorious appearing of the great God and our Saviour Jesus Christ" (Titus 2:11–13).

These three verses contain one of the neglected truths of the Bible. Probably no other passage in all of God's Word so completely summarizes the subject of Christian conduct. It does seem strange that this truth should be so neglected in a day when emphasis is placed on "practical Christianity" rather than doctrine. Unfortunately much so called practical Christianity is not the kind spoken of in these verses.

Three aspects of conduct are here mentioned. First. True Christian living denies ungodliness and worldly lusts. All things done apart from God, and the desire for the pleasures of this world as such, are thereby excluded. Second. Life should be lived godly, soberly and righteously in the present world. Third. The whole life should be lived in view of and with an expectation of the glorious appearing of Jesus Christ. Any "practical Christianity" that does not comprise these three conditions is not true Christian conduct. Present emphasis on "practical Christianity" seems to completely lack even mention of these three things as essential to Christian conduct. These three aspects of true conduct are considered more fully in later chapters.

Great as is the lack of emphasis upon that which constitutes true Christian conduct, there is even greater lack of emphasis upon that which teaches a believer how to live the true Christian life. The truth that the grace of God, the very same grace which brings salvation, also teaches those who are saved how to live pleasing unto God, seems to have been entirely overlooked by many. One who ·says, "I believe in grace, but I do not think it should be emphasized too much because that leads to careless living" has failed to understand God's work of grace on behalf of all He by grace has saved from wrath.

Even among those who accept grace as the only means of salvation, exclusive of any works or merit on the part of man, there is regrettable neglect of emphasis on the fact that the spiritual life can be sustained, developed, and brought to perfection *only* by the operation of the same grace. Growth in spiritual life comes only by the grace of God. Peter admonished, "Grow in grace" (2 Pet. 3:18).

There is great need for a fuller presentation of grace; not only of the truth that salvation from condemnation is entirely of grace, but even more of the truth that the very same grace which brings salvation also teaches the saved how to live "godly in this present world."

In the above passage, this teaching work of grace is emphasized. In the original text the meaning is: "to train up a child, to chasten, to instruct, to teach." The same word in Hebrews 12:6, 7 and 10 is translated by some form of the word chasten. Thus when grace teaches, it does more than impart knowledge as an instructor. It teaches in the sense that wise parents train and discipline children. This must first of all be in love, and not by threatenings. It is done by pointing out that which is good and helpful and warning against that which is wrong and destructive. It may mean withholding things that are greatly desired; but it also means giving encouragement, both by word and by actual help, in difficult times and in failures. Moreover, it includes chastening when necessary and this, as in Hebrews 12:6, may partake of the nature of scourging. But it never means forsaking the child.

All impartation of spiritual truth, all instruction, all reproof, all admonition, all exhortation, and all chastening are elements of the discipline by grace.

There is a false idea, a prevalent one, that God's law teaches men how to live godly lives. Does not the law set forth high standards of moral living that man may know how to live pleasing unto God? Not only unsaved men hold this view; but a vast majority of believers, in a greater or less degree, consent to it. This view is not in harmony with the passage under consideration.

Certainly, unsaved men are not taught righteousness by the law. If that were the purpose of the law, then it would have been one of the most colossal failures of all of God's economy, for it is said that by the law every mouth is stopped and all the world is guilty before God (Rom. 3:19). Not one man has learned godliness by the precepts of the law.

But was not the Mosaic Law given to God's people, Israel, to teach them the conduct He required of them? Truly, but in giving the law, God also with it provided sacrifices as a ground for extending mercy when they broke the law. This proves that God knew that the law could not so teach righteousness as to produce godly living.

Two errors had crept into the Galatian church. The one of these was that the justified believer is made perfect by keeping the law. Had this contention been true, it might rightly be said that the law is the teacher of godliness, but Paul in contending against this error wrote, "Wherefore the law was our schoolmaster to bring us unto Christ, that we might be justified by faith. But after that faith is come, we are no longer under a schoolmaster" (Gal. 3:24, 25). Notice, the law was our schoolmaster to bring us *unto* Christ. In other words, it is by the law and the failure to fulfill its demands that man is brought to Christ, who is the source of grace. When that has been done there is no further need for the law as a schoolmaster.

Another statement definitely affirms that the law is not a teacher of godliness. It is, "For sin shall not have dominion over you: for ye are not under the law, but under grace" (Rom. 6:14). By inference, he who is under the law is dominated or ruled by sin. From this it is clear that while God in the law sets forth standards of life for man, the law was not expected to produce righteousness in the lives of men. The reason is that the law merely tells men what they must do. Then it is left to man, entirely in his own strength, to do that which the law demands. Because of man's sinful nature this is impossible. That is why the law cannot be a means of producing godliness in man. This is confirmed by the words, "For what the law could not do, in that it was weak through the flesh" (Rom. 8:3).

It is therefore fundamental to recognize that all teaching of righteous living, to be effective, must not be grounded in law, but in grace. Any appeal for godliness, not related to grace is based on a false premise.

To reject the law as a teacher is not to say that there are no standards set for Christian conduct. Grace also sets standards but these are on a much higher plane. Those of the law are on a high human plane; those of grace on a divine plane. Furthermore, grace supplies that which is needed to live according to these ideals. Of the Holy Spirit, who is a gift of God's grace, Jesus said, "He will guide you into all truth" (John 16:13). He is not merely a sign post that points to high ideals. He is a divine Person dwelling in the believer to guide into "all truth." This is something entirely unknown to the law.

Jesus said, "I am come that they might have life, and that they might have it more abundantly" (John 10:10). He came "full of grace and truth" (John 1:14). The grace which came by Him gives spiritual life; also, by teaching, it makes that life more abundant.

Paul wrote to the Philippians, "I thank my God upon every remembrance of you. . . . Being confident of this very thing, that he which hath begun a good work in you will perform it until the day of Jesus Christ" (Phil. 1:3, 6). The beginning of the work was *saved by grace,* the performance of it is *disciplined by grace.* God never saves a person and then leaves him to himself to finish the good work. He Himself perfects that which He has begun. Grace is just as important, it is just as much needed, and is equally provided for both.

How wonderful it is, to know that the same grace, the same loving kindness of God, which sent His Son to the Cross and brought salvation, also disciplines and perfects that life which is born of God!

One more word, in the passage under consideration, requires attention. It is the little word us. Grace teaches us, not all men. Salvation bringing grace appears to all men, but only those who receive Him by whom grace came are taught thereby. The discipline of grace is not for the unsaved. They are "dead in trespasses and sins" (Eph. 2:1), and cannot be taught how to live until they have been spiritually born.

2

Grace Defined and Explained

THERE is much misunderstanding of grace. Few indeed seem to have grasped its true and full meaning. Grace never means a license to sin, as some seem to think. In fact, it is grace that prevents a believer from sinning. Because of this lack of understanding of grace, it is necessary to consider the true meaning thereof.

Grace, like truth, life, and light, is so great a term that it defies an all inclusive definition. The following is suggested as being helpful. Grace is the unmerited, abounding provision of the unrestrained operation of God's infinite love, through Jesus Christ; on behalf of man, especially those who depend upon Him.

The providence of God is His provision for the sustenance of the natural creation. Rain, sunshine, and the elements in the earth are part of His providence for plant life. Food for animals and all other things needed to sustain their lives are the gift of His providence. So also are food, clothing, shelter, and everything needed for the well being of man's natural life. All these are provisions by the Creator for the benefit of the created. God's providence for His creation, though partially withheld and limited by the curse because of sin, has never failed.

Grace is a similar great and abounding provision of God, but instead of being for the physical creation it is essentially for the spiritual realm. It is a provision of God to restore all that was lost spiritually because man sinned, and makes possible and sustains a new creation on a far higher plane than any other creation. Truly, grace is a great provision of God. It is summed up in these words: "He that spared not his own Son, but delivered him up for us all, how shall he not with him also freely give us all things?" (Rom. 8:32).

Grace is the operation of God's love. "For God so loved the world, that he gave his only begotten Son" (John 3:16). This giving of the Son in death for every man is said to be by the grace of God (Heb. 2:9). Those who received grace upon grace out of His fulness (John 1:16), are the same whom Jesus loved unto the end (John 13:1). To those who are chosen to be before Him in love (Eph. 1:4), God will in the ages to come show the exceeding riches of His grace (Eph. 2:7). In each of these, God's love is expressed by His grace. Grace is God's love in action.

God's love is infinite. "God is love" (1 John 4:16). As God is infinite so are His attributes. Therefore, that love which He is must be infinite. Again, God's love is infinite because the measure of it, His only begotten Son, is infinite. Thus the grace of God, flowing from infinite love, is inexhaustible. It can never fail.

Grace is unmerited. Man can contribute nothing to that which God does in grace, nor do anything to merit it. "And if by grace, then is it no more of works: otherwise grace is no more grace" (Rom. 11:6). "Now to him that worketh is the reward not reckoned of grace, but of debt" (Rom. 4:4). Therefore works, as a means of obtaining God's favor and grace, are completely excluded. God's grace always acts first on behalf of man, before man can act on behalf of God.

But grace is more than unmerited favor. It is favor toward those who deserve the very opposite. "But God commendeth his love toward us, in that, while we were yet sinners, Christ died for us" (Rom. 5:8). "When we were enemies, we were reconciled to God by the death of his Son" (Rom. 5:10). By the grace of God Jesus died for sinners—for His enemies. Sin, therefore, does not, in fact cannot, limit the grace of God. "But where sin abounded, grace did much more abound" (Rom. 5:20). In fact, sin made the manifestation of grace possible.

Grace is the unrestrained operation of love. While it is true that sin cannot limit God's infinite love, there is something, which also is infinite, that completely restrained it. This restraining force was the infinite justice of God, which demands that sin must be punished according to His holy law. Because of this, God was not free to do for the sinner all that His love desired. In order that love might operate freely and without restraint, something first had to be done to satisfy every demand of God's justice.

If God's justice were to be satisfied by the sinner, he must lose his life, for the law demands that the sinner must die. "The wages of sin is death" (Rom. 6:23). But if the sinner be put to death, no opportunity remains for love to operate in his behalf. It is clear then, that if God's justice was to be satisfied, and love left free to operate, God Himself had to supply that which was needed. That is exactly what happened in the cross. God's love found a way to satisfy His own justice and thereby set love free to operate without restraint. "Herein is love, not that we loved God, but that he loved us, and sent his Son to be the propitiation for our sins" (1 John 4:10). "And he is the propitiation [that which satisfies divine justice] for our sins: and not for ours only, but also for the sins of the whole world" (1 John 2:2).

Apart from the death of Christ, God cannot deal with fallen man on any other basis than law and justice. But when Christ died, the restraint upon God's love was removed and love set free to act. This removal of the restraint upon love is essential to grace. What a price, in suffering and shame, the Son of God paid, that God's love might be free to operate in grace!

Grace, then, is more than love; it is love operating righteously in view of the fact that the penalty for sin has been paid. Something was done for God on the cross. He became free to fully exercise His love, without compromising His justice.

Grace, therefore, is not the mere expression of pity or compassion on the part of God. It is not the setting aside of justice and passing over sins which should be punished. It is not a forbearance with sin. It is, let it be repeated, a forgiveness of sin because the full penalty has been paid by Another. This is basic to grace, and that upon which grace in its every aspect rests. Apart from the propitiatory death of Christ, there can be no grace of God toward men.

Love, then, did not disregard the law; it satisfied its every demand and fulfilled and established it, and then made possible a new way for God to deal with those who, by faith in His provision, have established the law. This new way is unrestrained love. It is grace. Believers are not under law because the penalty, which is the essence thereof, has been paid. They are under grace, an entirely new and different method by which God deals with man.

When God's justice has been satisfied once and for all, grace becomes sovereign and reigns unto eternal life.

Grace is on behalf of man, especially all who believe. Grace is the operation of God's love on behalf of *man*. Nothing in the Bible declares that God's grace operates on behalf of either the fallen or the unfallen angels. Grace seems to be reserved for man alone. There are two aspects to grace as it benefits every man. It was by the grace of God that

Jesus tasted death for every man, in order that
God's justice might be satisfied. So also, "The grace
of God that bringeth salvation hath appeared to all
men" (Tit. 2:11). Apart from these and the fact
that, during this age of grace, God withholds judgment upon the unsaved, His grace is only for believers in Jesus Christ. One of the basic acts of
God's grace is to justify the sinner. As this is conditioned upon faith in Jesus (Rom. 3:26), it follows
that God's grace operates, with the above exceptions, only on behalf of those who believe.

There is another statement which declares that
faith is a condition for the operation of grace. "It
is of faith, that it might be by grace" (Rom. 4:16).
Faith in Jesus Christ, then, is the condition for the
grace of God to operate on man's behalf.

Grace is through Jesus Christ. Grace comes only
through Jesus Christ. Apart from Him there is no
grace. "And of his fulness have all we received, and
grace for grace. For the law was given by Moses,
but grace and truth came by Jesus Christ" (John
1:16, 17). All things that are said to be of grace are
also said to be, in Christ, by Him, or through Him.
All spiritual blessings in the heavenlies are in
Christ (Eph. 1:3). In Him is redemption through
his blood, the forgiveness of sins according to the
riches of His grace (Eph. 1:7). He who believes is
"justified freely by his grace through the redemption that is in Christ Jesus" (Rom. 3:24). Because of
its inclusiveness in this connection, Romans 8:32
might well be quoted again: "He that spared not

his own Son, but delivered him up for us all, how shall he not with him also freely give us all things?" He who by faith receives the Son, receives with Him the gifts of grace.

Grace, then, is God's provision to bring into being, sustain, and perfect His new creation in Christ Jesus. It is the operation of His infinite love on behalf of such as are worthy of everlasting punishment. This outpouring of God's infinite love is possible only because Jesus Christ, by His death, fully satisfied all the demands of God's justice. As grace came by Jesus Christ, only those who receive Him are under grace.

3

Grace Upon Grace

I T IS not only important to know the meaning of grace; it is equally necessary to realize the extent to which grace enters into the believer's life. This is essential as a background for understanding the discipline of grace.

Many think of grace merely as the means whereby God forgives sin; and fail to recognize that grace is God's way of dealing with one who receives Christ, not only during the earthly existence, but also throughout eternity. Great harm has come from this limited conception of grace and the lack of teaching the fulness thereof. The present low level of Christian conduct is largely due to incomplete teaching of grace. All misconceptions on the part of many, that an over-emphasis on grace is a license to sin, would quickly be removed if grace were preached and understood in its fulness. "Grace and truth came by Jesus Christ" (John 1:17). Truth is inseparably related to grace. It is the result of grace because grace is that which God does and this must be truth. Only as grace enters into every phase of the believer's life, can there be truth in that life. "And of his fulness have all we received, and grace for [upon] grace" (John 1:16). It is grace upon grace that removes fear and gives assurance, stability and direction to the earthly life.

It has already been pointed out that it was by the grace of God that Jesus tasted death for every man, and that the grace of God that brings salvation, has appeared to all men. Because of this operation of grace, it is possible for every man to be saved, but only those who believe are saved. Salvation is by grace but through faith. "For by grace are ye saved through faith; and that not of yourselves: it is the gift of God" (Eph. 2:8).

As there are three aspects to salvation: from the penalty of sin, from the power of sin, and from the presence of sin; so there are also three aspects to grace. Grace gives a standing before God, grace provides for the daily life on earth, and there shall be an exceedingly great demonstration of grace in the ages to come.

By grace a standing before God. The first work of grace provides a standing before God. This is fully accomplished the moment a sinner believes on Jesus Christ as the One who satisfied, on his behalf, the demands of God's justice. The following are but some of the things that constitute the believer's standing and are accomplished by His grace. It is said that in Christ "we have redemption through his blood, the forgiveness of sins, according to the riches of his grace" (Eph. 1:7). All who believe are "justified freely by his grace through the redemption that is in Christ Jesus" (Rom. 3:24). Through disobedience and rebellion, in the Garden of Eden, the human race became enemies of God. Reconciliation has been made through the death of Jesus

Christ, which He tasted by the grace of God. "And you, that were sometime alienated and enemies in your mind by wicked works, yet now hath he reconciled in the body of his flesh through death" (Col. 1:21, 22). These and all other things that constitute the believer's standing, are directly or indirectly said to be by grace. The standing by grace is more fully considered in a later chapter.

Grace for the daily life. God's Word has much to say about the grace of God as it contributes to the earthly life of a believer. Every believer stands in grace and has access thereto by faith (Rom. 5:2). This alone is assurance that God is ready to act in grace in every circumstance of life.

What Paul said concerning himself should be the realization of every believer. "But by the grace of God I am what I am: and his grace which was bestowed upon me was not in vain; but I laboured more abundantly than they all: yet not I, but the grace of God which was with me" (1 Cor. 15:10). According to this, all that a believer is and every labor of love by him, is a result of the grace of God. Apart from His grace, nothing can be accomplished for God.

In reply to Paul's threefold prayer to be relieved from a "thorn in the flesh," God said, "My grace is sufficient for thee: for my strength is made perfect in weakness" (2 Cor. 12:9). Here God's grace sustained Paul at a time of great affliction. In this is seen the sufficiency of grace for all times and under all circumstances.

The grace of God delivers believers from the power of sin. "For sin shall not have dominion over you: for ye are not under the law, but under grace" (Rom. 6:14). It is only grace, God's infinite provision in love, that can break the power of cancelled sin, and set the believer free. How different this from the charge (which has its source in human reasoning) that an over-emphasis on grace might cause Christians to become careless! There is not too much grace teaching; but rather not enough.

Again, it is through grace that a believer becomes spiritually strong. Paul wrote to Timothy, "Thou therefore, my son, be strong in the grace that is in Christ Jesus" (2 Tim. 2:1). Thereby he would be able to endure hardness as a good soldier of Jesus Christ and so strive as to be crowned. Without grace it is impossible to win in the spiritual conflicts of life.

Closely related to the admonition to be strong in grace is another, "Be not carried about with divers and strange doctrines. For it is a good thing that the heart be established with grace" (Heb. 13:9). The alternative to a heart "established with grace" is a restless and fearful heart. That is the experience of vast numbers of believers who do not understand the abounding grace of God. Surely a believer's striving in his own power, with the accompanying failures, and the fears of possibly being lost, do not establish the heart. That causes uncertainty, distress, and fainting. But when it is seen that God's work of grace cannot fail, because it is of Him, and that back of His purpose is all His infinite power and grace, the heart does find rest and becomes established.

When the heart has been established by grace there is grace by which to serve God acceptably. "Wherefore we receiving a kingdom which cannot be moved, let us have grace, whereby we may serve God acceptably with reverence and godly fear" (Heb. 12:28). "And God is able to make all grace abound toward you; that ye, always having all sufficiency in all things, may abound to every good work" (2 Cor. 9:8).

One service for God is specially mentioned as being of grace. Paul, in writing to the Corinthian Christians, referred to the liberal contribution by the churches of Macedonia as the grace of God bestowed upon them. By this grace of God, though "in a great trial of affliction the abundance of their joy and their deep poverty abounded unto the riches of their liberality" (2 Cor. 8:2).

Paul spoke of his own preaching as being by the grace of God. He said, "Unto me, who am less than the least of all saints, is this grace given, that I should preach among the Gentiles the unsearchable riches of Christ" (Eph. 3:8). Not only his own preaching, but all ministerings to the Church, Paul declared to be of grace. "But unto everyone of us is given grace according to the measure of the gift of Christ." "And he gave some, apostles; and some, prophets; and some, evangelists; and some, pastors and teachers; For the perfecting of the saints, for the work of the ministry, for the edifying of the body of Christ" (Eph. 4:7, 11, 12).

Hebrews 4:16 exhorts, "Let us therefore come boldly unto the throne of grace, that we may obtain mercy, and find grace to help in time of need." Yes, there is a provision of God's infinite love to fully supply in time of need. This is by grace and grace alone.

"Now our Lord Jesus Christ Himself, and God, even our Father, which hath loved us, and hath given us everlasting consolation and good hope through grace, Comfort your hearts, and stablish you in every good word and work" (2 Thess. 2:16, 17). The benediction of grace is everlasting consolation and good hope issuing in comforted hearts and stability in good words and good work.

Surely all this and much more is grace upon grace for the believer's earthly life. There is nothing in life for which there is not grace. Because grace is so essential for every detail of the believer's life there can be no danger in teaching too much grace. The danger lies in not understanding grace and in not teaching it enough.

Grace in the ages to come. But the above does not exhaust grace upon grace of the fulness of Christ. Even more grace is to be brought at the revelation of Jesus Christ (1 Pet. 1:13). While not specifically said to be by grace, it is clear that the raising of those that sleep in Christ, the changing of believers who are alive, and the catching up together of all to be with the Lord throughout eternity (1 Cor. 15:52 and

1 Thess. 4:16, 17), must be a provision of infinite grace. Surely no one merits this final and glorious deliverance from the consequences and presence of sin. But even more, to be conformed to the image of the Son of God (Rom. 8:29); to be made like Him (1 John 3:2); having bodies fashioned like unto His glorious body (Phil. 3:21); being one with the Father and the Son even as they are one (John 17:21), and finally, sharing with Him the glory given by the Father (John 17:22); can only be brought about by the operation of the matchless grace of God. Nothing else can explain so great an exaltation of a creature that once was in rebellion and at enmity to God.

But as glorious as all this is, it does not exhaust the infinite and unrestrained provision of God's love. God's ultimate purpose in saving man is: "That in the ages to come he might shew the exceeding riches of his grace in his kindness toward us through Christ Jesus" (Eph. 2:7). Forgiveness of sins is according to the "riches of His grace" (Eph. 1:7); but the grace to be shown in the ages to come is the "exceeding riches of His grace." Only after the last vestige of sin, with its consequence death, has forever been done away, will the grace of God find its fullest manifestation. That surely will be the fulness of grace upon grace.

One passage sums up the entire work of grace. "Christ also loved the church, and gave himself for it; That he might sanctify and cleanse it with the washing of water by the word, That he might present it to himself a glorious church, not having spot, or wrinkle, or any such thing; but that it should be holy and without blemish" (Eph. 5:25–27). This expresses the meaning of grace upon grace. It is not only God's means of forgiving sin, but includes all that He does with and for the believer in raising him from his lost and condemned estate; in purifying and perfecting him; and finally, in placing him a glorious being, far above all other created beings, in a perfect union with Himself.

4

Denying Ungodliness and Worldly Lusts

IN ORDER to realize the true nature of that which grace teaches, it is important to know what ungodliness and worldly lusts are. Popular conception limits ungodliness to that which is wicked, immoral, depraved, debased, dishonorable, dishonest, and the like. That is not true. Much that is highly moral, cultured, and refined is as ungodly as are these things.

The word ungodly is defined as "not having regard for God." It includes all that is done without taking God into account. Many speak of the unsaved as ungodly, but fail to realize that everything that a saved person does without taking God into account is also ungodly. The saved are godly because of their standing in Christ, but many tolerate much ungodliness in their lives. Every act in a believer's life that does not take God into account is ungodly. Everything that one cannot ask God to bless is ungodly.

The true nature of ungodliness is best understood from man's relationship to God. Man came into being by a creative act of God (Gen. 1:27). Therefore, all that man is and all that he has, is of God. He Who created can also supply every need of the creature. Because the Creator is love, His care for the creature is assured. The only proper attitude of the creature toward his Creator is one of absolute dependence upon Him in all things. That necessitates taking God into account in every detail of life. Dependence upon the Creator is, then, the basic law for man; as it is for all of God's creation.

There is, however, a fundamental difference between man's dependence upon God and that of most of His creation. The whole universe depends upon God's provision for its maintenance. By Christ all things consist—are maintained and held together (Col. 1:17). The universe is made up of matter, having fixed properties. These properties respond to physical laws by which God controls and sustains all matter and energy. Because the material universe is inorganic its dependence upon the Creator is fixed and unalterable.

The vegetable kingdom also depends upon the Creator, and is governed by fixed laws. But these are laws of life by which light and heat are received from the sun, rain from the clouds, and elements out of the earth and air. All of these are provided by the Creator and received automatically by the plant. The animal kingdom likewise depends upon the Creator, and is preserved through natural laws. These laws are of a higher order and include instinct. All this speaks, in no uncertain terms, of creation's dependence upon God's bountiful provision; but all is of a reflex, or non-voluntary nature.

To the rational being man, created with power of choice and freedom of will, dependence upon God must include something far more than a mere non-voluntary reaction to fixed laws, or even instinctive action. To him, dependence upon God includes an understanding of His provision and an attitude of confidence and trust. Having freedom of will, his dependence must partake of the nature of a voluntary act. It must be a willing subjection of self to God, in recognition of His infinite resources and love. Because of his freedom to will, man can disregard God in his life and act independently of Him. In fact, because of the initial sin of man, it is a part of the very nature of man to do so.

The first test that came to man was a test of his voluntary dependence upon God (Read Gen. 3:1–7). The serpent said to the woman, "Yea, hath God said, Ye shall not eat of every tree of the garden?" This was a subtle question designed to raise doubt as to the fulness and goodness of God's provision. It implied that God was withholding some highly desirable thing. It was a direct attack upon man's recognition of full dependence upon his Creator, and his need to consider Him in all affairs of life. It was the first veiled suggestion that man might, to his own advantage, act independently of God.

The woman's reply to the serpent, the first recorded word of man, indicated that the initial step away from a voluntary dependence upon God had been taken. She said, "We may eat of the fruit of the trees of the garden: But of the fruit of the tree which is in the midst of the garden, God hath said, Ye shall not eat of it, neither shall ye touch it, lest ye die." Five words here were an addition to God's command and suggest a feeling of unnecessary restraint, and that His command was unreasonable. These words indicate a desire for greater self-expression. They also show that she had left the path of unquestioning faith and had resorted to reason. She had begun to look to her own intelligence, instead of the infinite wisdom of God.

Having departed from the path of unquestioning acceptance of God's Word, the woman was prepared for the serpent's next statement, "Ye shall not surely die." This was a direct denial of God's word. Then was added the greatest of all lies, "Ye shall be as God, knowing good and evil" (R.V.). This offer to be like God was an offer of independence of God; a freedom to choose and act according to the dictates of her own reason and desires. Henceforth it would not be necessary to consider God in all things.

Having exchanged faith for reason, and looking to self instead of to God, sedition had already taken place in the heart. This sedition was immediately sealed by the first recorded act of man. The woman took of the fruit and ate, and gave also to her husband and he ate. By this simple act, man declared his independence of God. The creature, who owed all to his Creator, rebelled against Him. The first ungodly act had been committed.

This spirit of independence of God became the very nature of man and, by heredity, has been transmitted from generation to generation; making the entire human race a rebel in God's universe.

Though man has rebelled against God, he has never established his independence. He is still dependent upon God, but unwilling to acknowledge it. It is an involuntary dependence, something akin to the dependence of animals, but in a spirit of rebellion.

The history of man from Adam to the present day is a history of dependence upon self and independence of God. He has been largely left out of man's thinking. Man has planned, acted, and lived as though God did not exist. All this is ungodliness.

Near the close of the pre-deluvian period Jehovah said, "My spirit shall not always strive with man" (Gen. 6:3). This indicates a general disregard for God. At Babel, shortly after the flood, men said, "Go to, let us build us a city and a tower, whose top may reach unto heaven; and let us make us a name" (Gen. 11:4). Here is no mention of anything vile, immoral, or debased. All shows great human progress, but all was of themselves, and for their own glory. Not taking God into account, their work was ungodly, and brought upon them the judgment of God.

Because the peoples of the earth had forsaken Him, God called Abraham out from his people into a land where God would bless him and his posterity; and raise up a people for His Own glory. But even they forgot God. Jehovah charged, "For Israel hath forgotten his Maker" (Hosea 8:14). And again, "they were filled, and their heart was exalted; therefore have they forgotten me" (Hosea 13:6).

So God, by the hand of Nebuchadnezzar, set aside

Israel as a ruling nation; and made him the first ruler of the Times of the Gentiles. But he also, as those before him, left God out of his plans. One day, walking on the walls of Babylon, he said, "Is not this great Babylon, that I have built . . . by the might of my power, and for the honor of my majesty?" (Dan. 4:30). Again, man in his accomplishments disregarded God. All was of self, by his own power and for his own glory. This, with very limited exceptions, has ever since been the spirit of Gentile rule over the world.

The great indictment brought by Paul against the ungodly human race is, "when they knew God, they glorified him not as God, neither were thankful; but became vain in their imaginations, and their foolish heart was darkened. Professing themselves to be wise, they became fools" (Rom. 1:21–22).

History reveals great human accomplishments made possible only because of God given intelligence. These in themselves were not ungodly; but because God has been left out of the thinking and planning and the glory has not been ascribed to Him, all of these works have been ungodly. The grace of God teaches all who by grace have received a new life, with a new divine nature, to deny all this ungodliness.

Grace also teaches us to deny worldly lusts. To lust is to long for and greatly desire something. Worldly lusts are things of the world which are longed for and desired because of selfish pleasure and gratification derived there-from. The world, or cosmos, is truly against God for it is the domain of Satan: "the whole world lieth in wickedness" (1 John 5:19). Though Satan, at times, comes as an angel of light (2 Cor. 11:14) and that which he has to offer may appear very attractive, all he does is for the purpose of drawing the believer away from God. As the believer fails to depend upon God and to take Him into account, the things of the world become attractive and there arises a desire for the pleasures derived from them.

The discipline of grace brings to the mind and soul the goodness and beauty of God, His unfailing love, and His all inclusive provision. When the heart sees this goodness of God and the riches of His grace; the pleasures, preferment, honor and wealth of the world lose their glamour. They are seen as temporal in contrast to the eternal values of God. The believer who realizes that through grace, and grace alone, he has been saved out of the lost and condemned world unto an indescribably glorious eternity with God sets his affection on things above—not on things of this earth. It is the work of grace to create and sustain this attitude.

Ethics can teach men to deny the dishonest, immoral, and debased things of this world; but grace alone can teach the believer to deny himself the beautiful, attractive, and pleasant things with which God is not identified.

By grace the believer has been called out of the ungodly world and delivered from the condemnation resting upon it. By grace he is also delivered from the desire for the things of the world, and his desires become centered in Christ and things of Him.

The teachings of grace do not compromise with the world nor permit careless living. Unfortunately some hold that there is a Christian liberty which permits participation in worldly pleasures. That is not liberty, it is license and is entirely at variance with the teachings of grace that worldly lusts should be denied. True Christian liberty is deliverance from the law of sin in the body with its desires for the pleasures of the world.

5

Teaching Us Godliness

G ODLINESS is defined as, "careful observance of, or conformity to the laws of God." This definition might, however, be misleading because a punctilious observance of God's law in self-effort and for personal honor becomes self-righteousness. The Pharisees were sticklers for the laws of God, but Jesus said that they were of their father, the Devil.

If, as already seen, ungodly means not to have regard for God; then godly means to have regard for Him, including voluntary dependence upon Him. A godly life is free from doubt as to His wisdom, His love, His goodness, and His provision. Dependence upon God excludes all dependence upon self.

A believer is dependent upon God in a twofold sense. When a person is born again, God does much more than reinstate him into Adam's original condition; he becomes a new creation, with a divine nature (2 Cor. 5:17). The creation of Adam was by the omnipotence of God. The new creation is not only by the power of God, but also by His sovereign grace, made possible by the death of His Son. This doubly guarantees God's ability and willingness to provide all that His new creation needs. "He that spared not his own Son, but delivered him up for

38

us all, how shall he not with him also freely give us all things" (Rom. 8:32). Herein is an unqualified assurance of provision for every need. Surely every child of God should exercise unfailing dependence upon His power and His love as expressed in His grace.

It is of the greatest importance to recognize that godly living includes this unfailing dependence upon the grace of God, as controlling in every aspect of life. The believer in Christ cannot be said to be living a truly godly life until he is brought to bow his head and heart to sovereign grace.

The humble attitude of complete dependence upon God is certain to express itself in a voluntary submission to His will; and the injunction "whatsoever ye do, do all to the glory of God" will become the rule of life. The little word "all" excludes from godly living even the least thing done to satisfy a desire for personal honor and glory. As God's purpose in saving man is to the praise of the glory of his grace, so the object of all godly living must also be to the praise of the glory of His grace. The Creator should be glorified by His works. Much more, when the Creator left His place in glory and died to save the creature from everlasting condemnation, should He be glorified by those who are saved.

That which measures up to high moral standards is not always godly living, although godly living will so express itself. The world religions have moral codes, but conformity thereto is not godly living. Conformity to the Golden Rule or to the Mosaic

law, would be godly living only if it could be in full
dependence upon God, and done to His glory. Pious
and puritanical living, however self-sacrificing, is
not necessarily godliness. A life in dependence upon
God will be marked by the absence of much of the
pleasure of the world and by many self-denials, but
the absence of these is not in itself a test of godliness.
It may be self-righteousness and spiritual pride.

Godly living is not mere service for others. The
present day social service program of neighborliness
and good will of many churches, if not in dependence upon God and if not for His glory, while of
temporal value, is not godliness.

That the believer's life should be in complete dependence upon God is taught in many different
ways.

The most simple statements thereof are: "The
just shall live by faith" (Heb. 10:38); without faith
it is impossible to please God (Heb. 11:6); "whatsoever is not of faith is sin" (Rom. 14:23). An understanding of the word faith is needed to bring out
the full meaning of these statements. One of the
clearest explanations of faith is found in Romans
4:18–21. Concerning Abraham it is said, "Who
against hope believed in hope, that he might become the father of many nations; according to that
which was spoken, So shall thy seed be. And being
not weak in faith, he considered not his own body
now dead, when he was about an hundred years old,
neither yet the deadness of Sarah's womb: He stag-
gered not at the promise of God through unbelief;

but was strong in faith, giving glory to God; And being fully persuaded that, what he had promised, he was able also to perform." Abraham was strong in faith because he was fully persuaded that what God had promised, he was able also to perform. Abraham's faith was a sublime dependence upon God to fulfill His promise. Faith in God, then, is complete dependence upon Him. Negatively stated, faith includes an emptying of oneself; of self-will, self-confidence, and self-effort.

But faith is more than trusting God to do things asked of Him; it is trusting Him to do whatever He in His infinite wisdom knows to be best, even if it is a denial of the thing asked. Some teach that all illness will be healed if only the sick person has enough faith in God. One who so teaches presumes to dictate to God what is best. This entirely ignores the fact that dependence upon God's wisdom is as important as dependence upon His power.

Faith is not a mysterious energy, emanating from within oneself, by which things are brought to pass. It is in no sense work; it is rather a cessation of work, or self-effort.

To live by faith is not to live by sight. To live by sight is to depend upon circumstances, such as a fine position, health, a bank account, friends, family ties and many other things. These are of great value to the believer, but to depend upon them and trust in them is not to walk by faith. To live by faith is also not to live according to reason. The essence of reason is dependence upon one's own intellect to plan and to provide. To substitute reason for faith in God is to trust one's own intellectual capacity more than God's wisdom and power.

"The just shall live by faith" means, the just shall live by dependence upon God.

Emphasis upon the faithfulness of God should be a great stimulus to dependence upon Him. "Faithful is he that calleth you, who also will do it" (1 Thess. 5:24). "He is faithful that promised" (Heb. 10:23). "Great is thy faithfulness" (Lam. 3:23). "Casting all your care upon him; for he careth for you" (1 Pet. 5:7). "But my God shall supply all your need according to his riches in glory by Christ Jesus" (Phil. 4:19). Surely the promises of God and His faithfulness teach complete dependence upon Him.

Practical sanctification also teaches complete dependence upon God. To sanctify is to set aside for a purpose. One who sanctifies himself unto God, sets his life aside for God's purpose. This act recognizes God's will as governing in that life, and this signifies dependence upon God. In his great treatise on sanctification, Paul used words which beautifully convey the idea of dependence, "yield yourselves unto God, as those that are alive from the dead, and your members as instruments of righteousness unto God" (Rom. 6:13). Yield is the key word to sanctification. In a yielded person there is no resistance to the will of God. There is no self-planning nor insistence upon one's own ideas or rights; but complete dependence upon God. The word instrument also signifies dependence. An instrument is in itself inactive; it depends upon someone to use it. The harp produces no melody until its strings are touched by the harpist's fingers. The surgeon's knife performs no operation until guided by the surgeon's skill. All instruments must be yielded to some master's touch to be of value. That is what Paul meant by "yield your members as instruments unto God."

Multiplied admonitions to pray are repeated reminders of the believer's dependence upon God. "Pray without ceasing" (1 Thess. 5:17). "I will therefore that men pray everywhere" (1 Tim. 2:8). "Praying always with all prayer and supplication in the Spirit" (Eph. 6:18). In prayer one expresses a need that he himself is unable to satisfy, and acknowledges dependence upon God to supply that which is needed. The essence of prayer is acknowledgment of helplessness coupled with confidence in God to supply the need. To pray without ceasing is to maintain a constant attitude of dependence upon God.

Paul admonished, "Giving thanks always for all things unto God and the Father in the name of our Lord Jesus Christ" (Eph. 5:20). Only one who is completely dependent upon God can give thanks always for all things. This is possible only as one has full confidence, not only in God's power and willingness but also in His love and wisdom to do that which is best at all times. There is no finer expression of dependence upon God than in giving thanks.

Prayer acknowledges one's dependence upon God

in time of need; thanksgiving acknowledges dependence when the need has been satisfied. Ten lepers prayed, "Master, have mercy upon us"; only one returned to give thanks. Nine forgot their dependence upon Jesus the moment they were healed.

And finally, the very nature of grace demands dependence upon God. "Therefore it is of faith, that it might be by grace" (Rom. 4:16). Grace being God's infinite and unmerited provision for every need, it is complete in itself without the addition of anything by man. It is only because of His grace that God asks man to live in dependence upon Him. Grace on God's part and dependence upon the part of man are inseparable. Therefore, godly living in this age is possible only under grace. That life which is in complete dependence upon God is not dominated by sin, because the essence of sin is dependence upon self instead of God. That is why Paul could write, "sin shall not have dominion over you: for ye are not under the law, but under grace" (Rom. 6:14).

To be completely dependent upon God and to desire to do His will and glorify Him are the basic principles of godly living. It is only by the discipline of grace that these characteristics are developed in a human life.

6

The Bread and the Wine

A<small>N EXPERIENCE</small> in the life of Abraham (See Gen. 14:17–25) beautifully illustrates the truth that the grace of God teaches believers to deny ungodliness and worldly lusts. It is noteworthy that this experience was by Abraham, who was called the "father of all them that believe," and of whom it was written, "he believed in the Lord; and he counted it to him for righteousness" (Gen. 15:6). This then was the experience of a believer; that which it illustrates ought to be the experience of every believer.

The story of Abraham and his nephew, Lot, is familiar to Bible readers. Because of a quarrel between their herdsmen, Abraham offered Lot the choice of any part of the land he wished. Lot chose the fertile plains before Sodom. Later, Lot was found dwelling in Sodom, even sitting in its gates. Then four kings came up against Sodom, overran it, and carried away the goods thereof. Lot also was carried away. Abraham, on learning of this, pursued the kings and smote them; and delivered Lot and all the people and goods of Sodom. By this victory Abraham had unintentionally become the benefactor of the king of the wicked city of Sodom. As Abraham returned from the slaughter of the kings, the king of Sodom went out to meet him and to reward him. Abraham was about to be tested.

At that very moment a third person, altogether unannounced, appeared upon the scene. He was Melchizedek, king of Salem: he brought bread and wine to refresh and strengthen Abraham after the hard battle. It is important to note that Melchizedek was not only king of Salem, he was also the priest of the Most High God.

The moment Abraham, the man of faith, was to be tested, God sent a priest to him. It was not a law-giver that God sent, nor was it a prophet to remind him of judgment that might come upon him if he departed from the way of righteousness. No, Melchizedek was neither of these; he was a priest. And why a priest? A priest is one who approaches God, on the basis of a sacrifice that has been made to atone for sin, and pleads with God on behalf of man. Because of the sacrifice, the demands of God's holiness and righteousness have been met, and therefore God is free to act in grace in response to the pleading of the priest. The sacrifices of the Aaronic priesthood given together with the law were, as has been mentioned, God's provision for showing mercy to those who broke the law. It was, then, the grace of God that came to Abraham in the person of Melchizedek. The whole incident was on the ground of grace—pure grace. It was grace disciplining Abraham.

But there is more here that speaks of grace; Melchizedek brought bread and wine. That bread and wine were a type, pointing forward to the death of Christ, just as now the bread and the wine are symbols reminding the believer thereof. Inasmuch as the death of Christ satisfied divine justice and made grace possible the incident clearly speaks of grace.

After the bread and the wine had been brought, Melchizedek blessed Abraham in the name of the Most High God, possessor of heaven and earth. The blessings of the "possessor of heaven and earth" were added to the benefits derived from partaking of the bread and the wine. As the bread and wine point to the Son, whom God spared not, but delivered up for us all, so the blessings of the possessor of heaven and earth point to the "all things" which are freely given with the Son (Rom. 8:32). Here then, is "grace upon grace." It was the grace of God which brings salvation, teaching Abraham that God, because He is the possessor of heaven and earth, is fully able to give him everything he needed. It was a reminder that the riches which God, who owns heaven and earth, gives are far greater than any possible favors from an ungodly king. God's gifts, being both spiritual and temporal, satisfy both the spirit and the body.

That Abraham responded to this teaching by grace is seen in that he gave tithes, of all that he possessed; his cattle, his gold, his grain, his silver, nothing was left out. It was out of a heart overflowing with devotion to the Most High God that Abraham gave tithes. There is not the slightest evidence of compulsion to do this act. The gifts of bread and wine and the blessings had been bestowed unconditionally. Abraham's tithes were given freely. In

this giving of the tithe, Abraham voluntarily ac-
knowledged his full dependence upon God for all
that he had. This is the true state under grace.

But Abraham was taught, not only to depend
upon God, but also to deny ungodliness and worldly
lusts. How well that was needed! Immediately after
Melchizedek had blessed him, he was approached by
the king of Sodom, who said, "Give me the persons,
and take the goods to thyself." Those goods were
the riches of the wicked city of Sodom; the very
riches by which Lot had been tempted. Those riches
were now, by the king himself, offered to Abraham.
That was a crucial moment for Abraham. Would he
become the friend of the ungodly king? Would he
accept at his hand unholy riches? Or, would he deny
the ungodliness and worldly lusts by refusing the
king's friendship and riches?

How well Abraham had been taught and fortified
against this temptation by his communion with
Melchizedek is seen from his prompt answer, "I
have lift up mine hand unto the Lord, the most
high God, the possessor of heaven and earth, That
I will not take from a thread even to a shoelachet,
and that I will not take anything that is thine, lest
thou should say, I have made Abraham rich."

Not a word of commandment had been spoken
to Abraham; not even an admonition. Communion
with God's high priest had revealed to Abraham the
riches of God's grace wherein He had abounded toward him. This had shown him the utter worthlessness of the riches of the ungodly king as compared

with the blessings of the Most High God. This shows that the mere reminder of what Christ has accomplished by His death and what God does in love because of Him is a tremendous force for separation from worldly lusts. It was not the riches as such that Abraham spurned. He already possessed great riches. He would not accept them at the hand of the ungodly king. He looked to God's abounding provision in love to supply all that he needed.

But notice, will you, the words that Abraham used in declining the proffered wealth. He said, "I will not take from a thread even to a shoelachet." Why a thread, and why a shoelachet? A thread is the smallest part of a garment. Garments in the Bible are symbolic of the believers' righteous standing before God. The shoelachet is that which holds the shoe fast, and aids in walking. The earthly life of the believer is called his walk. The meaning of this, then, is that the world cannot contribute the smallest particle, neither to the believer's standing before God nor to his holy living.

As Melchizedek brought bread and wine to Abraham, so Another, "Called of God a high priest after the order of Melchizedek" (Heb. 5:10), also took bread and wine. When He took the bread and brake it, he said, "Take, eat: this is my body, which is broken for you" (1 Cor. 11:24). He also took the wine, and said, "this is my blood . . . which is shed for many for the remission of sins" (Matt. 26:28). Ever since, throughout this age of grace, the bread and the wine have been a memorial to all believers;

a constant reminder of what God in grace, through Christ, has done for them.

As Abraham was strengthened by the bread and the wine and the communion with Melchizedek; so likewise is the believer strengthened in meditation upon what Christ is to him, as symbolized by the bread and the wine. Thereby he is able to spurn the proffered riches and pleasures of the world. A vision of Christ, of his broken body and shed blood, prompts the believer to refuse to be enriched by the ungodly world. The realization that God is the possessor of heaven and earth, and that He is able to supply all need according to His riches in glory by Christ Jesus (Phil. 4:19), makes it possible to reject the favors of the world. It is when the truth of Romans 8:32 (quoted above) grips the life, that the importance of the riches of the ungodly world lose their attractiveness. The Son, "delivered up for us all" is the guarantee that He who gave the Son, He who is the possessor of heaven and earth; shall also give all things needed for this earthly life.

This experience in the life of Abraham is, then, a perfect picture of the discipline of grace to the exclusion of anything related to the law. Abraham was a believer. Melchizedek, the high priest, is a type of Christ by whom came grace and truth. The bread and the wine are types of the broken body and shed blood of Christ by which God was made free to act in grace. The blessing in the name of the Most High God points to full provision in grace for the believer's every need. In the giving of the tithes is seen the believer's acknowledgment of complete dependence upon God. The spurning of the wealth proffered by the wicked king is a denial of all worldly lusts as unable to contribute anything either to the believer's standing before God or to his godly life.

7

To Do Thy Will, O God

THIS earth has seen but one truly godly Life. An examination of that Life reveals true godliness. When the Son of God came into the world He said, "Lo, I come to do thy will, O God" (Heb. 10:9). This was His purpose in coming! All other purposes were but details of this His supreme purpose. Throughout His earthly life, He never deviated therefrom.

The Father's will was always the controlling motive of His life. To His disciples, when they asked Him to eat, He said, "My meat is to do the will of him that sent me, and to finish his work" (John 4:34). Later, to the Jews, He said, "I seek not mine own will, but the will of the Father which hath sent me" (John 5:30); and again, "I came down from heaven, not to do mine own will, but the will of him that sent me" (John 6:38). As He faced the greatest of all issues of His life, He prayed, "O my Father, if it be possible, let this cup pass from me: nevertheless not as I will, but as thou wilt." A second time He prayed, "O my Father, if this cup may not pass away from me, except I drink it, thy will be done." He prayed a third time saying the same words (Matt. 26:39, 42, 44). Truly, "being found in the fashion as a man, he humbled himself, and became obedient unto death, even the death of the cross" (Phil. 2:8).

From His purpose to do the will of God He never wavered. Here was one Man who always honored the supreme authority of the will of God. Being God and not a creature, He of all beings might have claimed the right to exercise His own will; but He voluntarily chose to be subject to the will of the Father. What a contrast to the creature man who desired to become like God and be free to act according to his own will.

In full harmony with His declaration that He had come to do the will of God, He constantly proclaimed that He had been sent by Him. "I proceeded forth and came from God; neither came I of myself, but he sent me" (John 8:42). No less than forty times in John's gospel is mention made of the fact that the Father had sent Him. That was His authority for all that He said and did. It was also an acknowledgment of His dependence upon the Father.

But even more, He ascribed all His works and words to His Father. When the Jews charged Him with breaking the law by healing an impotent man on the Sabbath, He said, "Verily, verily, I say unto you, The Son can do nothing of himself, but what He seeth the Father do: for what things soever he doeth, these also doeth the Son likewise" (John 5:19). Before healing a man born blind, He said, "I must work the works of him that sent me" (John 9:4).

At the feast of Tabernacles He declared, "My

doctrine is not mine, but his that sent me" (John 7:16); and another time He said, "I have not spoken of myself; but the Father which sent me, he gave me commandment, what I should say, and what I should speak" (John 12:49).

He was always conscious of the fact that it was not His own life that was being expressed by Him, but the very life of the Father. He said, "I live by the Father" (John 6:57).

His dependence upon God is further seen in the frequency and intensity with which He prayed. He prayed when He was baptized by John (Luke 3:21). Before choosing His twelve disciples, He "went out into a mountain to pray, and continued all night in prayer" (Luke 6:12). After times of special effort He prayed. Having healed the multitudes, "he withdrew himself into the wilderness and prayed" (Luke 5:16). After an evening in Capernaum, healing and driving out devils, "rising up a great while before day, he went out, and departed into a solitary place, and there prayed" (Mark 1:35). Having fed five thousand men, beside women and children, He went up into a mountain apart to pray (Matt. 14:21, 23).

To Peter, after having foretold his denial of Him, He said, "I have prayed for thee, that thy faith fail not" (Luke 22:32). In the upper room He prayed for His disciples and for all who through their word should believe on Him (John 17:20). Three times he prayed on His own behalf in the garden of Gethsemane (Matt. 26:36, 39, 42, 44); and on the cross He prayed for His enemies, "Father, forgive them;

for they know not what they do" (Luke 23:34).

He prayed always with full assurance of being heard. At the grave of Lazarus He said, "Father, I thank thee that thou hast heard me. And I knew that thou hearest me always" (John 11:41, 42). There can be no greater trust than this.

In many other ways Jesus expressed His dependence upon the Father and an unfailing consciousness of oneness with Him. "As the Father knoweth me, even so know I the Father" (John 10:15). "I and my Father are one" (John 10:30). "I am not alone, because the Father is with me" (John 16:32). The realization of His intimate relationship with the Father contributed to His perfect dependence upon Him. .

This dependence was for one supreme purpose— that the Father be glorified in Him (John 7:18). Having finished His ministry of grace, He said to the Father, "I have glorified thee on the earth. I have finished the work which thou gavest me to do" (John 17:4).

He always lived in full dependence upon God: even so, as He drew His last breath on the cross He said, "Father, into thy hands I commend my spirit" (Luke 23:46).

He who was co-equal and co-existent with God, He whom the Father loved before the foundation of the world, He who with the Father created man, He who came forth from the bosom of the Father, He who became the instrument for the expression of the Father's infinite love for a lost world, He by whom came grace and truth: He it was who took upon Himself the form of the creature in order to express true dependence upon God and to perfect a pattern for godly living.

Shortly before His departure from the earth He said to His disciples, "As my Father hath sent me, even so send I you" (John 20:21). Surely this commission must include a life lived according to the pattern which He gave. Grace, and grace alone, teaches how to so live.

8

The Trial of Faith

BECAUSE the attitude toward God under grace should be complete dependence upon Him, it follows that the teachings of grace must include that which will perfect and purify this dependence. Such a provision is found in suffering. That, in fact, seems to be the greatest reason for suffering by God's people. Even the Son of God Himself, as the Captain of salvation, was made perfect through suffering. Through intense suffering in Gethsemane, His unfailing dependence upon the Father found its fullest expression in the words, "not my will, but thine, be done" (Luke 22:42).

That suffering is God's method under grace for perfecting and purifying faith is taught in the following: "now for a season, if need be, ye are in heaviness through manifold temptations: That the trial of your faith, being much more precious than of gold that perisheth, though it be tried by fire, might be found unto praise and honour and glory at the appearing of Jesus Christ" (1 Pet. 1:6, 7). It is the trial of faith, not works nor accomplishments for Him, that is said to be unto praise and honor and glory at His appearing.

When Peter wrote these words he surely had in mind the trial of his own faith at the trial of Jesus.

57

Shortly before Jesus with His disciples went out into the Garden, He said to Peter, "Simon, Simon, behold, Satan hath desired to have you, that he may sift you as wheat: But I have prayed for thee, that thy faith fail not." To this Peter had answered, "Lord, I am ready to go with thee, both into prison, and to death" (Luke 22:31–33).

Did Peter's faith fail? Did he not deny his Lord? Certainly he denied his Lord, but if it be said that his faith failed, then Jesus' prayer for him was not answered. Was that possible? How then can this be understood? Was it in faith that Peter made his boasting profession of faithfulness? It seems not. His words, "Although all shall be offended, yet will not I" (Mark 14:29), are full of self-confidence. Peter's failure, then, was of self; not of his faith in God. Through this failure Peter learned his own weakness and inability to carry out his own resolve. This is the first essential for dependence upon God. Out of this experience, though painful and disgraceful, Peter emerged with a deeper sense of need of his Lord and greater faith in Him. Before his fall, Peter had faith in Jesus as the Son of the living God; but this faith was mixed with much confidence in self. By the trial of his faith, confidence in self was burned out and his faith in the Son of God included dependence upon Him for his daily life. In permitting Peter to fail because of confidence in self, grace taught him to depend wholly upon God.

As in Peter's case, so with all believers, failure of

the flesh may be God's means to bring about a greater dependence upon Him that blossoms into an enriched spiritual life. Failures due to dependence upon self should be stepping stones to deeper spiritual experiences.

Paul had a great trial of faith. Of it he wrote, "And lest I should be exalted above measure through the abundance of the revelations, there was given me a thorn in the flesh, the messenger of Satan to buffet me, lest I should be exalted above measure. For this thing I besought the Lord thrice, that it might depart from me. And he said unto me, My grace is sufficient for thee: for my strength is made perfect in weakness. Most gladly therefore will I rather glory in my infirmities, that the power of Christ may rest upon me" (2 Cor. 12:7–9). Paul had not failed to depend upon Christ, but because of the great revelations given him, such as no other man had ever received, he might possibly think of himself as important. This trial was sent to keep him in humble dependence upon God.

The trial of faith, then, is not a testing as to whether or not there is faith, nor if the faith is sufficient; but rather a purifying of faith, a removal of all impurities of dependence upon self. That this was in the mind of Peter is clear from his comparison with the trial of gold by fire. As in the heat of the fire the dross is separated from the pure gold, so in the heat of trial and suffering the things of the world, in which so much confidence is placed, are

burned away and God alone is left as the object of
dependence. This, then, explains many of the trials
and sufferings of God's people.

The pure faith that emerges from the trial of
faith is said to be more precious than gold tried by
fire. In the sight of God pure faith in Him, uncon-
taminated by confidence in self, has a high value.
If one should pass through a great trial in life and
not come out with a deepened realization of dependence upon God, then something of vastly
greater worth has been lost than any temporal loss
sustained by that trial.

The purpose of the trial of faith is that the purified dependence upon God might be found unto
praise and honor and glory at the appearing of Jesus
Christ. This strongly suggests that just as the faith of
Abraham and of all believers in Jesus Christ is
counted unto them for righteousness (Rom. 4:22–
24); so the purified faith, which by manifold trials
has been cleansed from every particle of dependence
upon self, shall be counted unto believers for praise
and honor and glory. Both the imputed righteousness and the praise, and honor and glory are entirely
apart from works. All is because of dependence upon
God in response to His grace.

But why should God attach so much importance
to the trial of faith? To understand this it is necessary to look far back into the past and then follow
through the course of human history. At a time,
long before man was created, Lucifer, full of wisdom
and perfect in beauty, was the covering cherub on

the holy mount of God. He was probably the highest of all of God's creatures and apparently was next to God Himself. He was perfect in all his ways until iniquity was found in his heart (Ezek. 28:12–15). His iniquity consisted in a five-fold ."I will" culminating in "I will be like the Most High" (Isa. 14:13, 14). This was the first time that any creature set himself up against the Creator and refused to maintain an attitude of complete dependence upon Him. Lucifer's "I will" was a willful refusal to remain subject to God and to depend upon Him in all things.

Later, man was created in the image of God. He too was made perfect. He was the crowning work of God's creation, and to him was given dominion over the earth and all that was upon it. Being a creature of God, his only rightful attitude, as previously explained, should have been complete dependence upon his Creator. But he too refused to remain in that position. On the promise, by the Serpent, that he would become like God, man disobeyed God and departed from the state of simple and complete dependence upon Him.

The history of mankind has been one long record of self-sufficiency and doing without God. This condition will continue until it culminates in the Man of Sin, the son of perdition, "Who opposeth and exalteth himself above all that is called God, or that is worshipped; so that he as God sitteth in the temple of God, shewing himself that he is God" (2 Thess. 2:4).

But there is another side, a bright side, to this great panorama of the ages. There was Another who came upon the scene. It was even He who said, as He came into the world, "Lo, I come to do thy will, O God." That was His purpose in coming. He "was manifested, that he might destroy the works of the devil" (1 John 3:8). All the works of the devil have their root in the two words "I will," and his greatest work is to destroy man's dependence upon God. The Son of God came to do away with this and to restore man to a complete and willing dependence upon God.

God's purpose then in the lives of His children while here on earth is to create, develop, strengthen, and refine that complete dependence upon Him which must be found in those who, throughout all eternity, are to be the very closest to Him and share His glory: they who are to take a place nearer to Him even than that held by Lucifer before he declared his independence of God.

That is why God places so great emphasis upon the trial of faith. He is preparing for Himself a new creation in Christ Jesus that will be in complete voluntary dependence upon Him and in loving subjection to Him. The purpose of grace is, through suffering, to discipline the child of God and produce this state of dependence upon the Father.

9

Grace Teaches Humility

DEPENDENCE upon God produces humility in man. Pride and boasting are traits of natural man, and spring from man's dependence upon self and self-sufficiency. Whatever success comes to man tends to feed and nourish his pride. These traits, though not always obvious, are very persistent and are also evident in the lives of those who are saved. There is a deep rooted desire to be something. If not openly, yet in the heart persists a feeling of self-importance.

This feeling of pride is out of harmony with God's program of grace, for grace emphasizes the fact that everything is of God. "For who maketh thee to differ from another? and what hast thou that thou didst not receive? now if thou didst receive it, why dost thou glory, as if thou hadst not received it?" (1 Cor. 4:7). "And base things of the world, and things which are despised, hath God chosen, yea, and things which are not, to bring to nought things that are: That no flesh should glory in his presence" (1 Cor. 1:28, 29).

The only condition placed upon man for the enjoyment of all the blessings of grace is faith, "it is of faith that it might be by grace" (Rom. 4:16). This law of faith, of simple dependence upon God in order to receive His blessings of grace, cuts under man's proneness to think highly of himself and so excludes boasting. "Where is boasting then? It is excluded. By what law? of works? Nay: but by the law of faith" (Rom. 3:27). Paul's attitude was, "God forbid that I should glory, save in the cross of our Lord Jesus Christ" (Gal. 6:14). The glory of the cross lies in the fact that because of it God is free to act in grace toward man.

The cross and grace which flowed from it produced in Paul a deep humility which caused him to say, "I am the least of the apostles, that am not meet to be called an apostle. . . . But by the grace of God I am what I am" (1 Cor. 15:9, 10).

But the grace of God taught Paul a still deeper degree of humility. The revelation of the fullness of grace and the call to proclaim the gospel of grace caused him to say, "Unto me, who am less than the least of all saints, is this grace given, that I should preach among the Gentiles the unsearchable riches of Christ" (Eph. 3:8). Here is a rare degree of humility, produced by the truth, which God fully revealed to him; "That the Gentiles should be fellow heirs [with the Jews], and of the same body, and partakers of his promise in Christ by the gospel" (Eph. 3:6). This body is nothing less than the body of which Christ is the head.

This, the greatest expression of God's grace, had never before been revealed to man. God had promised that the head of the Serpent should be bruised by the Seed of the woman (Gen. 3:15). In the sacrifices, He had made provision for extending mercy when the law was broken. He had repeatedly promised deliverance to Israel and also deliverance of creation from the curse upon it because of sin. Even more, the Son of God had become man and died on the cross for the redemption and reconciliation of man. In all these is salvation, and all is because of the grace of God. But, great as all this is, nothing herein does more than remove the consequences of sin and restore to man that which was lost by Adam's sin. This salvation does not change man from his status as man.

The truth revealed through Paul, that both Jews and Gentiles are fellow heirs, and of the same body, and partakers of the promise in Christ is infinitely greater than any concept of salvation that God had ever before made known to man. It is as much higher than salvation from the penalty and consequences of sin and to restoration to Adam's original sinless condition as heaven is above earth, as God is higher than man. That sinful and rebellious man, after having the sin question settled, is elevated to the very same order as the Son of God is the cardinal truth of the mystery revealed to Paul. This is the "unsearchable riches of Christ."

Paul, contemplating the marvels of grace in bringing sinful man into this exalted position, felt his own worthlessness and utter inability to contribute anything toward the accomplishment of God's purpose. Overwhelmed by this grace of God he became nothing in himself, and cried out, "who am less than the least of the saints."

As one stands at the foot of Niagara and beholds the great mass of water rushing over the precipice, he becomes awed by the greatness and power thereof and feels his own smallness. As one travels hundreds of miles along ranges of the snow and glacier clad Rocky Mountains and sees peak after peak rising thousands of feet high, and then tries to think back through the millenniums they have stood there, that too is not without an intense sense of one's own limitations. So David felt when, centuries ago, he went out into the night and, looking heavenward, said, "When I consider thy heavens, the work of thy fingers, the moon and the stars, which thou hast ordained; What is man, that thou art mindful of him? and the son of man, that thou visitest him?" (Ps. 8:3, 4).

If God's creative work, the work of His fingers, can so instill humility into man's soul, how much more will not His saving work of grace do so—that work which demanded for its accomplishment the death of His Own Son.

Paul, appealing for humility, said, "Let this mind be in you, which was also in Christ Jesus: Who, being in the form of God, . . . made himself of no reputation, and took upon him the form of a servant, . . . and being found in fashion as a man, he humbled himself, and became obedient unto death, even the death of the cross" (Phil. 2:5–8).

While on earth Jesus gave His disciples an example of humility. By washing their feet, He, the Creator and their Master, performed the menial act of the lowest servant. Having done this He admonished them to do likewise to each other.

The record of this act of self-humiliation (John 13:1–15) is preceded by two statements, usually overlooked, but absolutely essential to the very doing of the act. Both speak of things closely related to grace. The first describes Jesus' love for His disciples, "having loved his own which were in the world, he loved them to the end," or to the uttermost. Here is an unfailing love. His divine love prompted the act of self-humiliation. Nothing less than love could have done it, and remember, grace has its roots in divine love.

The second statement is, "Jesus knowing that the Father had given all things into his hands, and that he was come from God, and went to God." Notice carefully the emphasis on His knowledge of these things. To separate this knowledge of His relationship to the Father from the act is to rob it of its motive and enablement. Because He knew that he had power from God, that He had come from God, and that He was going to God He was able to so humble Himself. But all this speaks of grace; power by God, life from God and a future with God.

When Jesus asked His disciples to follow His example He did not expect them to do so without the same incentive and enablement which was His. Nor need any believer be without these great influences for humility.

Jesus' great commandment to his disciples was, "That ye love one another; as I have loved you, that ye also love one another" (John 13:34). This is possible only because the Holy Spirit indwells all believers and is there to shed the love of God abroad in the hearts (Rom. 5:5). Paul appeals for humility on the basis of love in these words, "If there be . . . any comfort of love . . . in lowliness of mind let each esteem other better than themselves" (Phil. 2:1, 3).

Jesus knew that the Father had given all things into His hands. Can the believer know the same? Certainly, as far as the power needed to do all God asks him to do. Paul said, "I can do all things through Christ which strengtheneth me" (Phil. 4:13). This he said in connection with "I know how to be abased." Paul not only knew of God's enabling power for himself, but also realized that all believers need to know that there is infinite power acting on their behalf. He wrote to the church at Ephesus that he did not cease to pray for them that they might "know . . . what is the exceeding greatness of his power to us-ward who believe, according to the working of his mighty power, Which he wrought in Christ, when he raised him from the dead, and set him at his own right hand in the heavenly places, Far above all principality, and power, and might, and dominion, and every name that is named, not only in this world, but also in that which is to come" (Eph. 1:18–21). Nowhere is found a finer description of God's infinite power. Nothing less than omnipotence is said to be "us-ward who believe." But most believers do not know this and have need of the prayer of some Paul that they might know it.

Jesus knew that He had come from the Father. True self-humiliation is not a trait of fallen man. The very essence of the first sin, a desire to be like God, was an effort at self-exaltation. As self-humiliation demands a divine nature, he who is to follow the example of Jesus must know that he has come from God. This is possible for all believers, for they are born of God (John 1:13). The apostle John said, "we know that we are of God" (1 John 5:19).

Jesus knew that He was going to God. Can every believer know the same? Yes, and that on the infallible and unfailing word of the Lord. He said, "I will come again, and receive you unto myself" (John 14:3). And again, in His intercessory prayer, Jesus declared, "Father, I will that they also whom thou hast given me, be with me where I am" (John 17: 24). There need be no uncertainty about this.

In the measure that one becomes possessed by the knowledge that he has come from the Father and that his eternal destiny is with Him, things of the world fade into insignificance. As pride has its roots in a desire to be something in the world, the devaluation of the things of the world produces humility.

Humility, then, is fostered by a deep sense of complete dependence upon God; by a realization of the infinitely glorious position in Christ; by the love of God shed abroad in the heart by the Holy Spirit; by a realization of the infinite power of the

Father on one's behalf, and by a certain knowledge that one is born of God and has an eternal destiny in the presence of and in union with the Father and the Son. It is the work of grace, and grace alone, to impart these glorious truths to the soul and thereby teach humility.

10

The Believer's Standing and State

CERTAIN Bible passages, especially in the Pauline letters, seem to contradict each other. One verse speaks of a thing as being fully accomplished while another refers to it as in process of completion. Heb. 10:10 reads, "we are sanctified through the offering of the body of Jesus Christ once for all." This is a finished work. In 1 Thess. 5:23 Paul wrote, "And the very God of peace sanctify you wholly." Here sanctification is an uncompleted process. Again Heb. 10:14 reads, "For by one offering he hath perfected forever them that are sanctified." Against this is Paul's admonition, "Be perfect" (2 Cor. 13:11). Why should those who have been perfected forever be told to be perfect? More illustrations might be given, but these are sufficient for the present purpose.

These seeming contradictions vanish when one understands that in each case the first verse refers to the believer's standing in Christ, or his position before God. He is positionally sanctified, or set apart for God's eternal purpose. He is perfect in God's sight because he is in Christ. In each case the second verse refers to the believer's life on earth which is called his walk, or state. His earthly life should be wholly set apart for God's use. He should live perfectly before God.

The believer's standing then is that position in which God has placed him and as God sees him because he has accepted Jesus Christ as Saviour. It is God's acceptance of him in Christ and as a member of the household of God. The believer's state is the condition of his earthly life. It is the expression, or lack of expression, of his spiritual life in and through his earthly body. It is the sum total of his experiences and, when in accordance with God's plan, is made up of communion with God, joy, peace, fellowship, labor of love for God and fellow man, and fruit bearing for God. To whatever degree these things are lacking the state is out of harmony with the standing. The purpose of the discipline of grace is to harmonize the state with the standing which is perfect and unchangeable.

It is not necessary to consider here all that enters into the believer's standing before God but only enough to show that this standing is infinitely great and wonderful, that it is unalterable, and that man does not contribute the least toward it. An understanding of these things is imperative to an understanding of the discipline of grace.

The broadest and most inclusive statement of that which takes place when one enters into a position in Christ is found in these words, "Who [God the Father] hath delivered us from the power of darkness, and hath translated us into the kingdom of his dear Son" (Col. 1:13). This is nothing less than being taken out of the realm over which Satan holds sway and placed in the realm of the Son of God.

From the moment a person believes in Jesus Christ as his Saviour, while still in it, he is no more of the world (John 17:11, 14). This is a change of the greatest possible significance.

The standing before God of all who are of this world is that of aliens and enemies to God (Col. 1:21); but all who are of the kingdom of the Son of God have been reconciled to God. "When we were enemies, we were reconciled to God by the death of His Son" (Rom. 5:10). They have also been made nigh to God. "But now in Christ Jesus ye who were sometimes far off are made nigh by the blood of Christ" (Eph. 2:13). They are now "no more strangers and foreigners, but fellowcitizens with the saints, and of the household of God" (Eph. 2:19).

To accomplish this great change from being without God (Eph. 2:12) to the closest and most intimate position held by any creature, several things must be done by God. All of these become efficacious the moment a person believes.

First of these to be mentioned is redemption from "under the law" (Gal. 4:5). "Christ hath redeemed us from the curse of the law, being made a curse for us" (Gal. 3:13). This redemption was with the "precious blood of Christ" (1 Pet. 1:19). "There is therefore now no condemnation to them that are in Christ Jesus" (Rom. 8:1 R.V.).

Together with redemption from under the law, there is complete forgiveness of all sins committed against that law. "In whom [Jesus Christ] we have redemption through his blood, the forgiveness of sins, according to the riches of his grace; Wherein he hath abounded toward us in all wisdom and prudence" (Eph. 1:7, 8). The purging of sins is specifically said to be by the Son Himself (Heb. 1:3). This complete forgiveness of sins against the law must not be confused with the forgiveness of sins against God the Father, which is conditioned upon confession (1 John 1:9). The first is part of the standing; the second is related to the state.

Another element of the believer's standing, directly related to redemption, is justification. "Being justified freely by his grace through the redemption that is in Christ Jesus" (Rom. 3:24). This is a free gift, made possible by the righteousness of Jesus Christ and because He "bare our sins in his body on the tree" (1 Pet. 2:24). "For he [God] hath made him to be sin for us, who knew no sin; that we might be made the righteousness of God in Him" (2 Cor. 5:21). Justification is more than forgiveness of sins. It is to be in Jesus Christ, clothed in His righteousness; standing before God as though one had never sinned.

The standing includes the relationship of a child to his Father. "But as many as received him [the Son of God], to them gave he power to become the Sons of God. . . . Which were born, . . . of God" (John 1:12, 13). Here is a spiritual relationship with God by birth as real and unchangeable as the relationship by physical birth of a child to an earthly father. But it is more, the life by the spiritual birth is eternal life. "He that believeth on the Son hath eternal life" (John 3:36 R.V.). This eternal life is the gift of God through Jesus Christ our Lord (Rom. 6:23). When one remembers that "the gifts . . . of God are without repentence" (Rom. 11:29), it is clear that the believer's standing before God is for time and eternity.

One who is a child of God is also an heir of God. "Wherefore thou art no more a servant, but a son; and if a son, then an heir of God through Christ" (Gal. 4:7). The Father has made all believers "meet to be partakers of the inheritance of the saints in light" (Col. 1:12); and has given the Holy Spirit as an earnest (i.e. a guarantee) of this inheritance (Eph. 1:14). Every believer has been made accepted in the beloved Son of God (Eph. 1:6); and is "complete in him, which is the head of all principality and power" (Col. 2:10).

In addition to all this, believers are the object of God's unfailing care. "While we were yet sinners, Christ died for us. Much more then, being now justified by his blood, we shall be saved from wrath through him. For if, when we were enemies, we were reconciled to God by the death of his Son, much more, being reconciled, we shall be saved by his life" (Rom. 5:8–10). The life of the Son by which the believer shall be saved, is not His earthly life, but that which He now lives in heaven at the right hand of the Father. Being saved by that life is said to be "much more" than being reconciled by

His death. This must mean that God's provision for the care and bringing unto glory of believers is much more than His provision for their justification and reconciliation unto Himself.

In addition to being objects of God's care, all who are His Own are objects of His never failing love. "For I am persuaded, that neither death, nor life, nor angels, nor principalities, nor powers, nor things present, nor things to come, Nor height, nor depth, nor any other creature, shall be able to separate us from the love of God, which is in Christ Jesus our Lord" (Rom. 8:38, 39).

A careful study of all these statements concerning the believer's standing before God will reveal that all is said to be of God and all is through Jesus Christ. In no case is room for any contribution on the part of man. The only condition placed upon man is to believe. As faith is dependence upon God, it adds nothing to that which God does. It merely gives Him the opportunity to work.

It is also evident that all the above, except the unfailing care and love of God, is declared to be a finished work, and not something in process of completion. Deliverance from the power of darkness and translation into the kingdom of God's Son are fully accomplished. So also are, redemption, forgiveness of sins, justification, being born of God, the receipt of the gift of eternal life, being made heirs of God, being accepted in the beloved, and being complete in Him. In no case is there the least suggestion that anything can be added to or taken from that which has been done.

This standing before God has been sealed by the Holy Spirit of God until the day of redemption of the body (Eph. 4:30). The seal denotes a finished transaction (Jer. 32:10), also security, and an unalterable position (Dan. 6:17; Rev. 20:3).

While the believer's standing is in no way conditioned upon his state there is, however, a close relationship between the two. The standing makes the state possible. One must be born of the Spirit before he can live a spiritual life. It is impossible to live pleasing unto God while dead in trespasses and sins and in rebellion against Him. There must first be reconciliation and acceptance in the Beloved.

The method of grace in teaching (to be more fully considered later) is to point to the things which God has done in providing the standing before Him and then pleading for a life in harmony therewith. It follows, then, that the standing must be completely provided by God and must exist in its full realization before God can use it as an incentive to a godly state.

It also follows that the standing must be perfect in every detail. This excludes all possibility of any fallible human contribution. To hold that "the state is necessary in order that the standing shall ultimately be realized" is to insist on adding human merit to God's perfect work, and to destroy the absolute perfection of that which God uses as an argument to promote a state that is acceptable to Him.

It is impossible to clearly understand God's work of grace in saving from condemnation and in teaching one who has been saved unless it is seen that the standing depends in no way upon the state, but the state rests entirely upon the standing.

11

Standards of Grace Teaching

THE DISCIPLINE of grace cannot be understood
without a clear conception of the high standards of life which God desires in those who are
taught by grace. Not only among those who constitute Christendom as a whole, but also among many
true believers, the ideals of Christian conduct are
largely limited to high moral standards. That this
is true is shown by the fact that emphasis is primarily upon the attainment to high ideals, the
prompting to noble endeavor, and the call of duty.
Moral conditions as such are stressed and that entirely apart from the believer's position in Christ.
This is on a purely human level. But these by themselves are not God's standards for life under grace.
It is entirely possible for natural man to learn to do
much that is good; not only because he must, but
also because he chooses to do so. He can be honest,
concientious, diligent, kind, loving, manly, self-con-
trolled, chaste, courteous, self-sacrificing, and seek
the welfare of fellow men, all because he esteems
these as virtues and is esteemed because of them.
Man can learn to resist the baser things of life by
the sheer power of his natural self. All of this is
most admirable in the life of any person and many
Christians would be much more useful if they pos-

sessed more of these qualities, but these alone do
not measure up to the high standards of life taught
by grace.

The purpose of grace is to produce in the believer
a life on the divine plane. It is far more than char-
acter building. Because the divine life is expressed
through the human body, the expression thereof
may be similar or even identical with the expression of the finer qualities of a natural human life.
Two persons may contribute to the welfare of their
fellow men. In the case of one, it may be the expression of a purely human life; to gain favor with
others, from a sense of fulfilling an obligation, or
even because of pleasure derived thereby. In the
case of the other, it is because the love of God has
been shed abroad in the heart. In each case the outward expression is the same, but to God there is a
vast difference. The one is a life in self-determina-
tion and for personal gain. The other is in dependence upon God and is a result of the teachings
of grace. False cults place great emphasis on the
finer qualities of human conduct.

The apostle Paul said, "And if I bestow all my
goods to feed the poor, and if I give my body to be
burned, but have not love, it profiteth me nothing"
(1 Cor. 13:3, R.V.). The life produced by the teachings of grace has the outward manifestations plus
the right attitude toward God.

While the outward expression of godly living, as
taught by grace, cannot always be distinguished
from the finer human life, there are standards of

godly living that are beyond the conception of the natural mind. These are on a divine plane, and therefore of a far higher order than the very finest teachings of the best philosophers, and moral teachers. The standards under grace are so high as to render comparison impossible, except by contrast, with even the highest standards of the great world religions. They are even higher than the high standards of the God given Mosaic Law.

All standards of conduct under the law were summed up in the two commandments, "Thou shalt love the Lord thy God with all thy heart, and with all thy soul, and with all thy mind"; and "Thou shalt love thy neighbor as thyself" (Matt. 22:37, 39). But that love for God is only on a human level. It is with a human heart, soul, and mind. To love one's neighbor as oneself is also only human because the love of self is human.

All standards of a life under grace are summed up by Jesus in the words; "This is my commandment, That ye love one another, as I have loved you" (John 15:12). Paul repeated this thought, "And walk in love, as Christ also hath loved us, and hath given himself for us an offering and a sacrifice to God for a sweetsmelling savour" (Eph. 5:2). The love of Christ for the believer is a divine love and was even unto death. When the believer is called upon to love as Christ loved, he is asked to love with a divine love—nothing less.

The Golden Rule says, "All things whatsoever ye would that men should do to you, do ye even so to them" (Matt. 7:12). Grace teaches, "let each esteem other better than themselves" (Phil. 2:3). "Let this mind be in you, which was also in Christ Jesus: Who, being in the form of God . . . made himself of no reputation, and took upon him the form of a servant" (Phil. 2:5–7).

The very thinking of one under grace should be in perfect harmony with the divine will, "bringing into captivity every thought to the obedience of Christ" (2 Cor. 10:5). If every thought is brought into the obedience of Christ there can be no wrong conduct, for conduct has its source in thought.

In the following verses are standards of life which rise far above moral conduct. "Giving thanks always for all things unto God and the Father in the name of our Lord Jesus Christ" (Eph. 5:20). "Be careful for nothing; but in everything by prayer and supplication with thanksgiving let your requests be made known unto God" (Phil. 4:6). "Rejoice evermore" (1 Thess. 5:16). "As sorrowful, yet always rejoicing" (2 Cor. 6:10). "My brethren, count it all joy when ye fall into divers temptations" (Jas. 1:2). "But rejoice, inasmuch as ye are partakers of Christ's sufferings" (1 Pet. 4:13). To be thankful for all things and to rejoice at all times, even in suffering, are not human characteristics. They are part of a divine life and are taught only by grace. "Forgiving one another even as God for Christ's sake hath forgiven you" (Eph. 4:32), is perfect forgiveness, because God's forgiveness for Christ's sake is "according to the riches of his grace; Wherein he hath abounded toward us in all wisdom and prudence" (Eph. 1:7, 8).

Natural man may develop great liberality in giving, but there is a kind of giving which is brought about only by the work of grace. It is described as follows: "Moreover, brethren, we do you to wit of the grace of God bestowed on the churches of Macedonia; How that in a great trial of affliction the abundance of their joy and their deep poverty abounded unto the riches of their liberality. For to their power, I bear record, yea, and beyond their power they were willing of themselves; Praying us with much entreaty that we would receive the gift, and take upon us the fellowship of the ministering to the saints" (2 Cor. 8:1–4). To give liberally, with great joy, when in deep poverty and suffering affliction, is not a standard for natural man, nor under law; it is only for a life under grace.

Paul prayed for the Ephesian saints that they "might be filled with all the fullness of God" (Eph. 3:19). As this prayer includes all believers, it is a standard for all who are under grace. When Paul joyfully accepted suffering and persecution that thereby the life of Jesus might be made manifest in his body, it was a manifestation of the fullness of God in him.

These are standards taught by grace and grace alone. No moral code, not even the Mosaic law, can demand them. Here is no room for careless living. These standards grant no license to violate the moral code because they are on an infinitely higher plane. One whose thoughts are kept in obedience to Christ and who is filled with all the fullness of God does not break the moral laws of God.

These standards do not set aside the value of the lower standards of the moral code, they include them as elements, just as a word includes letters, but in reading, attention is centered on the words which convey the meaning, not on the elements, that is the letters. So the law, called the letter, does not give meaning to spiritual life. That is by the Word that "dwelt among us, full of grace and truth" (John 1:14). There is no life in the letter, "for the letter killeth, but the spirit giveth life" (2 Cor. 3:6). He by whom came grace and truth said, "the words that I speak unto you, they are spirit, and they are life" (John 6:63).

12

By the Power of God

IT is difficult for many to grasp fully the truth that salvation from the penalty of sin is the work of God and of Him alone. All God does in redeeming, reconciling and justifying man and in giving him a new eternal life, is of God alone. Man can contribute nothing thereto. Difficult as this is for man to see, it seems even more difficult for the saved to realize that the life which God expects them to live is not of themselves, but by His Own power. Because of this lack of understanding, many believers strive in their own strength for high ideals of moral conduct, instead of yielding themselves to the power of God which will enable them to live according to the high divine standards under grace. When these high standards of life under grace are seen to be on a divine plane, it becomes evident that something more than human resources is needed. Divine power alone can produce a divine order of life.

The fact that the true life under grace is one of complete dependence upon God is evidence that that life must be lived by the power of God. If that life could be lived in the power of the believer, it would become a life of dependence upon self and not in dependence upon God.

In the teachings of grace great emphasis is placed

upon the fact that it is God Who works. "For it is God which worketh in you both to will and to do of his good pleasure" (Phil. 2:13). "Now the God of peace . . . Make you perfect in every good work to do his will, working in you that which is well pleasing in his sight" (Heb. 13:20, 21). "So then neither is he that planteth anything, neither he that watereth; but God that giveth the increase" (1 Cor. 3:7). In writing about spiritual gifts and the true ministry Paul said, "And there are diversities of operations, but it is the same God which worketh all in all" (1 Cor. 12:6).

Furthermore, to show that the power of the life under grace is of God, special emphasis is placed upon the weakness of man. "But we have this treasure in earthen vessels, that the excellency of the power may be of God, and not of us" (2 Cor. 4:7). "But we had the sentence of death in ourselves, that we should not trust in ourselves, but in God" (2 Cor. 1:9). "Not that we are sufficient of ourselves to think any thing as of ourselves; but our sufficiency is of God" (2 Cor. 3:5).

The admonition "yield yourselves unto God, as those that are alive from the dead, and your members as instruments of righteousness unto God" (Rom. 6:13) shows that the power is of God and not of man for the instrument is powerless apart from the master's control. This makes it important to distinguish between trying to serve God and being used of God. It should also be recognized that God does not desire to *help* believers do things for

Him; He desires to do the work Himself through them. Because grace is that which God, and He alone, does the true life under grace has all its sources in Him. It follows then that whenever there is failure in the life of a saved person it is due to de-pendence upon self, instead of God. This does not relieve the believer of responsibility for his life, but that responsibility is to yield to the control of God.

While salvation is of God, it is through Jesus Christ; so also godly living which is of God is through Jesus Christ. Jesus said, "without me ye can do nothing" (John 15:5). He also said, "As the living Father hath sent me, and I live by the Father: so he that eateth me, even he shall live by me" (John 6:57). And Paul said, "I live; yet not I, but Christ liveth in me: and the life which I now live in the flesh I live by the faith of the Son of God, who loved me, and gave himself for me" (Gal. 2:20). He also said, "I can do all things through Christ which strengtheneth me" (Phil. 4:13). "Nay, in all these things we are more than conquerors through him that loved us" (Rom. 8:37). "But thanks be to God, which giveth us the victory through our Lord Jesus Christ" (1 Cor. 15:57). "Now thanks be unto God, which always causeth us to triumph in Christ, and make manifest the savour of his knowledge by us in every place" (2 Cor. 2:14). Paul admonished believers to be "filled with the fruits of righteous-ness, which are by Jesus Christ, unto the glory and praise of God" (Phil. 1:11); and to "be strong in the Lord, and in the power of his might" (Eph. 6:10).

All of these passages clearly teach that attainment to the high divine standards of the life under grace is something more than to determine in the heart, as Daniel did, not to be defiled by the meat of the King's table. They can only be accomplished through the Lord Jesus Christ. It is impossible to live the true life under grace apart from Him. The popular idea that Christ goes alongside of the believer to lead, does not adequately describe His presence and work. He is in, not merely with all who believe in Him.

The divine way of life is not imposed upon the believer from without; it flows out from within as naturally as a spring. It is the outflowing of the indwelling Holy Spirit of God from the inner-most being of the believer. Jesus said, "He that believeth on me, as the Scriptures hath said, from within him shall flow rivers of living water. But this spake he of the Spirit, which they that believe on him were to receive: for the Spirit was not yet given; because Jesus was not yet glorified" (John 7:38–39 R.V.).

It is clear, then, that godly living is not merely a suppression of the desires of the natural man. In the seventh chapter of Romans, Paul described the struggle and failure in a life where an effort to suppress the evil is the controlling principle. He said, "For that which I do I allow not: for what I would, that do I not; but what I hate, that do I." "For I know that in me (that is, in my flesh) dwelleth no good thing: for to will is present with me; but how to perform that which is good I find not. For the good that I would I do not: but the evil which I would not, that I do" (vs. 15, 18, 19). Then he exclaims, "O wretched man that I am! who shall deliver me from the body of this death" (v. 24). But he also answered this question, "I thank God through Jesus Christ our Lord. . . . For the law of the Spirit of life in Christ Jesus hath made me free from the law of sin and death. . . . That the righteousness of the law might be fulfilled in us [it is in us, not by us] who walk not after the flesh, but after the Spirit" (Rom. 7:25 and 8:2, 4). To the Galatians Paul wrote, "Walk in the Spirit, and ye shall not fulfill the lusts of the flesh" (Gal. 5:16). "But the fruit of the Spirit is love, joy, peace, longsuffering, gentleness, goodness, faith, meekness, temperance" (Gal. 5:22–23). Notice that these things are the fruit of the Spirit. Fruit is not by a law that restricts and restrains, it is by a law of life within.

These passages all teach that godly living is the natural result of the operation of the indwelling Holy Spirit. It is just as natural as fruit growing on a tree. When fruit is not evident, there are things in the life which hinder the operation of the law of the spirit of life in Christ Jesus.

Peter attributed to the Spirit the purification of the souls in obeying the truth (1 Pet. 1:22). And Paul attributed all the things that Christ wrought by him to the power of the Spirit of God, and prayed for all believers that they might "be strengthened with might by his [the Father's] Spirit in the inner man" (Eph. 3:16).

The true life, then, which is taught by grace is not, as is so commonly thought, a life lived by the individual with some assistance from God at crucial times; but is rather a life of God Himself, by Jesus Christ, His Son, through the power of the indwelling Holy Spirit. It is manifested in those who are yielded to God and are willing to do His will.

13

Devotion and Works

THE expression "service for others" is very popular these days, not only in church groups, but also in luncheon clubs and other organizations. Emphasis on service as the primary, if not only, purpose of both moral and Christian conduct is often accepted without question. While service may be the highest ideal in purely moral and humanitarian conduct, that is not true of the Christian life. Nevertheless service, or good works, is a large part of God's purpose for those who are saved by grace. "For we are his workmanship, created in Christ Jesus unto good works, which God hath before ordained that we should walk in them" (Eph. 2:10). Therefore, any believer whose life is not filled with good works fails to measure up to God's purpose for him.

Paul, whose life was a constant labor of love, admonished his fellow believers, "my beloved brethren, be ye stedfast, unmovable, always abounding in the work of the Lord, for as much as ye know that your labour is not in vain in the Lord" (1 Cor. 15:58). And again, "I beseech you . . . brethren . . . that ye present your bodies a living sacrifice . . . which is your reasonable service" (Rom. 12:1).

The importance of works is further shown by the fact that God holds everyone responsible for what he does. "So then everyone of us shall give account of himself to God" (Rom. 14:12). "Wherefore we labour, that, whether present or absent [from the body], we may be accepted of him. For we must all appear before the judgment seat of Christ; that everyone may receive the things done in his body, according to that he hath done, whether it be good or bad" (2 Cor. 5:9, 10).

Repeated assertions that God recognizes good works is further evidence of their great importance. "If any man serve me, him will my Father honour" (John 12:26). "For God is not unrighteous to forget your work and labour of love, which ye have shewed toward his name, in that ye have ministered to the saints, and do minister" (Heb. 6:10). "Every man shall receive his own reward according to his own labour" (1 Cor. 3:8). "Knowing that whatsoever good thing any man doeth, the same shall he receive of the Lord, whether he be bond or free" (Eph. 6:8). "And, behold, I come quickly; and my reward is with me, to give every man according as his work shall be" (Rev. 22:12).

Surely all of these: God's purposes in saving man in order that he may perform good works, that every man is held accountable to God for what he does, and that God will not fail to recognize every good thing that is done, show the importance of service for God.

Devotion to Christ is most important. As important as are good works in the believer's life, there is that which in God's sight is even more important.

While Christ desires and recognizes service, He far more desires and values love and devotion to Himself. In this day when service has become the keynote of Christianity, meditation on Christ, devotion to Him, and a desire for Him, purely because of what He is, have almost become a lost practice. These are, however, necessary and prerequisites to acceptable service for Him.

An event in the lives of two sisters, among His most intimate friends while on earth, gave Jesus occasion to express Himself in this matter. The story is here quoted in full. "Now it came to pass, as they went, that he entered into a certain village: and a certain woman named Martha received him into her house. And she had a sister called Mary, which also sat at Jesus' feet, and heard his word. But Martha was cumbered about much serving, and came to him, and said, Lord, dost thou not care that my sister hath left me to serve alone? bid her therefore that she help me. And Jesus answered and said unto her, Martha, Martha, thou art careful and troubled about many things: But one thing is needful: and Mary hath chosen that good part, which shall not be taken away from her" (Luke 10:38–42).

These sisters represent two different attitudes that believers may take toward Christ. Both were intensely interested in Jesus, but there was a vast difference in their attitude toward Him. Martha's attitude was to do some material service for Him. She carried this so far that she became cumbered by "much serving" and as a result impatient with her sister. Martha considered service for Jesus as all important. Notice carefully, Martha was not occupied with things apart from Jesus, all she did was for Him. Mary, instead of doing something for Him, sat at His feet and received from Him.

To fully realize the situation, remember that their Guest was the One by whom all things had been made. He was the Word made flesh, full of grace and truth. He had come that out of His fulness of grace they might receive grace upon grace. Mary desired to receive spiritual things from Him, Martha was so busy in her task of serving Him with temporal things that she had no time to receive the spiritual things He had come to offer her.

In no uncertain words, Jesus expressed His estimate of these two attitudes toward Him. He kindly rebuked Martha for being careful and troubled about many things, and added that Mary had chosen that good part, which should not be taken away from her.

By His answer to Martha, Jesus announced that an attitude of devotion with a desire to receive from Him is more highly valued by Him than service with temporal things.

When Jesus gave His last commission to Simon Peter (John 21:15–17) He intensified His estimate of devotion over service. He made love for Him the condition for service. He said, "Simon, son of Jonas, lovest thou me more than these?" When Simon answered, "Yea Lord; Thou knowest that I love thee," Jesus said, "Feed my lambs." Three times Jesus with a slight variation repeated his question and three times Simon replied in the affirmative. The last two times Jesus commissioned him to feed His sheep. There can be no question here but that Jesus makes love for Himself the condition for ministering spiritual things to His sheep.

In a third instance the importance of the attitude toward Christ as over service, is set forth even more strongly. On the Island of Patmos John was commanded to write letters to seven churches in Asia Minor. To the church of Ephesus he was told to write, "These things saith he that holdeth the seven stars in his right hand, who walketh in the midst of the seven golden candlesticks; I know thy works, and thy labour, and thy patience, and how thou canst not bear them which are evil: and thou hast tried them which say they are apostles, and are not, and hast found them liars: And hast borne, and hast patience, and for my name's sake hast laboured, and hast not fainted" (Rev. 2:1–3). Notice carefully this fine commendation. They had works and labor and patience. They could not bear evil and had cast out false leaders. A second time they were commended for their patience and for their labor, even in the name of Christ; and in all this they had not fainted. Few churches indeed, in this age of emphasis on service, are worthy of this commendation.

But notice now even more carefully the admonition, "Nevertheless I have somewhat against thee, because thou hast left thy first love. Remember therefore from whence thou art fallen, and repent, and do the first works; or else I will come unto thee quickly, and will remove thy candlestick out of his place, except thou repent" (Rev. 2:4, 5). Only one thing was lacking in the church at Ephesus; it was the "first love" for Christ, a love for Him before everything else. Because of this they were warned that their candlestick would be removed out of its place if they did not repent. Apart from their first love they could not hold forth the light of the gospel of the grace of God. Surely there is something vastly more important to Christ than service, as important as that is.

From these three instances, it is clear that the Lord Jesus Christ desires and values the love of those who are His far more than any service they can possibly render Him. His love craves a response of love and adoration. "We love him, because he first loved us" (1 John 4:19).

14

Works Acceptable Unto God

THE good works which are an important part of God's purpose for every believer are acceptable to Him only under certain conditions.

Love must be the motive. It was only after Peter had confessed his love for Him that Jesus commissioned him to feed His lambs and His sheep. The church at Ephesus was warned that unless it returned to its first love its candlestick would be removed. It follows, then, that works, to be acceptable to Christ, must spring from love for Him. Love becomes the motive for all service for God. That is why Paul commends the saints at Thessalonica for their "labour of love . . . in the sight of God and our Father" (1 Thess. 1:3).

As "we love him, because he first loved us," basically it is the love of Christ as expressed in His death for sinners that must be the great motivating force in all true Christian activity. This was Paul's motive. He said, "For the love of Christ constraineth us" (2 Cor. 5:14). He also admonished, "walk in love, as Christ also hath loved us, and hath given himself for us" (Eph. 5:2).

Love must be the motive for all things done in response to grace. All that God does in grace is because of His infinite love; all is unmerited and given

freely. The response to this cannot be the fulfillment of a duty because no condition accompanies
the offer of God's free gift except faith. It cannot be
a return payment because that would be the payment of a debt. It cannot be to gain the good will
of God because grace is absolutely unmerited favor.
If it were necessary to do anything to assure a believer's final salvation, that which was so done would
be for personal gain and would not be motivated
by love. The fact that under grace God gives all
things freely excludes every other motive but love.

Everything done apart from love has no value in
the sight of God. Paul said, "If I speak with the
tongues of men and of angels, but have not love, I
am become sounding brass, or a clanging symbol.
And if I bestow all my goods to feed the poor, and
if I give my body to be burned, but have not love,
it profiteth me nothing" (1 Cor. 13:1, 3 R.V.). Because love is so essential to good works, Paul prayed
that the saints "being rooted and grounded in love,
May be able to comprehend . . . what is the
breadth, and length, and depth, and height; And to
know the love of Christ, which passeth knowledge"
(Eph. 3:17–19).

Fear is a false motive. A sinister influence, often
offered as a motive for Christian conduct, is fear:
fear of God's vengeance on the day of Judgment, of
being lost, of being forever cast out by God unless
certain standards of life, often man made, are maintained. This may take the form of fear of supposed
punishment or purging as a condition for final en-

trance into heaven. This motive of fear is used to restrain persons from doing that which is wrong or to encourage good deeds and contributions to the church. While not always so recognized, all this is appeasement offered to God.

Fear is the dominant motive in the world religions because these know nothing of the love of God that is in Christ Jesus. But fear is often a motive in the lives of multitudes of Christians who do not fully understand that love and the grace of God for them.

Fear is a desire to avoid or flee from that which causes harm. It is the natural feeling produced by the instinct of self-preservation. Self-preservation depends upon self to preserve; but he who sees, in grace, God's loving care for His Own, and places his trust in Him, does not rely on self-preservation. Then fear is banished.

That fear has no place in the life of a believer is clearly taught. "For God hath not given us the spirit of fear; but of power, and of love, and of sound mind" (2 Tim. 1:7). "Herein is our love made perfect, that we may have boldness in the day of judgment: because as he is, so are we in the world. There is no fear in love; but perfect love casteth out fear: because fear hath torment. He that feareth is not made perfect in love" (1 John 4:17, 18).

Must be a voluntary and joyful service. Because the motive for service for God is love, that service must be voluntary. That which is done because of love is never done grudgingly and surely not because of any compulsion except that which springs

from within, from one's own earnest desire to do all
that is done. It should never be thought of as a duty
performed nor as a responsibility fulfilled. The believer's labor of love does not partake of the nature
of the work of a servant for his master. That is not
the relationship between the Lord and those who
are His. Jesus, in His farewell talk to His disciples,
said, "Henceforth I call you not servants . . . but
I have called you friends" (John 15:15). This perfect friendship does not measure the labor ren-
dered nor expect payment in return. It is without
thought of gain or reward. The difference between
the work of a servant and of a friend is well expressed in these words, "But now we are delivered
from the law . . . that we should serve in newness
of spirit, and not in the oldness of the letter" (Rom.
7:6).

To Paul this newness of spirit had a real meaning.
He was able to say, "But none of these things [bonds
and afflictions that awaited him at Jerusalem] move
me, neither count I my life dear unto myself, so
that I might finish my course with joy, and the ministry, which I have received of the Lord Jesus, to
testify the gospel of the grace of God" (Acts 20:24).
The same spirit was found in the churches of Macedonia when "in a great trial of affliction the abundance of their joy and their deep poverty abounded
unto the riches of their liberality" (2 Cor. 8:2). True
labor of love is not only voluntary service but also
joyful.

Service under grace must be voluntary. Inasmuch as grace gives everything freely, out of the promptings of God's love, anything that the recipient of grace does for God, must be of his own free will.

Admonitions denote a voluntary compliance. All admonitions in the apostolic epistles are in words that clearly denote a voluntary response. Beseech was a favorite word with Paul. John and Peter also used it. "I beseech you . . . that ye present your bodies" (Rom. 12:1). "I beseech you . . . that ye all speak the same thing, and that there be no divisions among you" (1 Cor. 1:10); "we beseech you . . . that ye study to be quiet, . . . to work with your own hands, . . . that ye walk honestly" (1 Thess. 4:10–12).

That the word beseech is free from any suggestion of compulsion is clear from the fact that it has always been used in addressing God. "We beseech thee, O Lord God" is an appeal for voluntary response on His part. God uses the very same word in His appeals to believers to live pleasing unto Him.

Two other words frequently used are exhort and admonish. Though more authoritative than beseech, they still allow voluntary compliance. They exclude the idea of compulsion. To the church at Thessalonica Paul wrote, "As ye know how we exhorted and comforted and charged everyone of you, . . . That ye would walk worthy of God, who hath called you unto his kingdom and glory" (1 Thess. 2:11, 12).

The most common expression used is the little word let. It also implies freedom of will to comply or not comply. Only a few references can be quoted. "Let not sin therefore reign in your mortal body" (Rom. 6:12). "Let us not be desirous of vain glory" (Gal. 5:26). "Let us not be weary in well doing" (Gal. 6:9). "Let him that stole steal no more" (Eph. 4:28). "Let all bitterness, and wrath, and anger, . . . be put away from you" (Eph. 4:31). "Let the word of Christ dwell in you richly" (Col. 3:16). In all of these the appeal is for voluntary compliance.

From the above it is clear that Christ does not seek a forced, slavish, or coercive service. He desires a voluntary and joyous labor of love that issues from the heart.

Must be as unto the Lord. Good works are not only voluntary and joyful, being motivated by love; but they must be as unto Christ to be acceptable unto God. Christ died "that they which live should not henceforth live unto themselves, but unto him which died for them, and rose again" (2 Cor. 5:15). "Whatsoever ye do, do all to the glory of God" (1 Cor. 10:31). "And whatsoever ye do in word or deed, do all in the name of the Lord Jesus" (Col. 3:17).

The admonition is not only that good works be done unto the Lord Jesus Christ but also that they be not done as unto men. "And whatsoever ye do, do it heartily, as to the Lord, and not unto men . . . for ye serve the Lord Christ" (Col. 3:23, 24). These words written to servants (in fact slaves) concerning their service for human masters, make it clear that every detail of a believer's work, though done for the benefit of fellowman, should always be done as unto Christ.

It follows, then, that much so called Christian activity cannot be acceptable unto God. It is possible, even where sound doctrine is held, to find much activity that, by the foregoing tests, cannot be honored by God. It is done for personal preferment or because of a desire for recognition. Do not purely selfish motives too often actuate Sunday School, young peoples, and church workers? God alone knows what is actuated by the love of Christ, and is a voluntary labor of love for Him and unto His glory. That only is acceptable unto Him.

15

God's Ways and Man's Ways

"F OR my thoughts are not your thoughts, neither
are your ways my ways, saith the Lord" (Isa.
55:8). In no instance is this more true than in connection with promptings to proper conduct. Because under grace God does everything apart from
human merit and thought of repayment, He cannot
offer His blessings as an inducement, nor His judg-
ments as a threat to encourage godly living. Therefore, under grace God first reminds of what He has
done in grace; then on the basis of that, He appeals
for a life in harmony with that which He has done.

But man's ways are not God's ways. In general
man clings to the idea that benefits always come
because of good conduct and losses because of bad
conduct. Natural man always feels that he must
contribute something to earn God's favor.

God's method under grace is seen in Jesus' dealing with the woman, taken in adultery, and brought
to Him by the Pharisees. When the Pharisees had
gone out, having been silenced by Jesus, He said
to her: "Woman, where are those thine accusers?
hath no man condemned thee? She said, No man,
Lord. And Jesus said unto her, Neither do I condemn thee: go, and sin no more" (John 8:10, 11).
Jesus first freely forgave her sin, for which under

the law she was worthy of death; then He admonished her to live a life free from sin.

It is important to recognize that under the law God's order was reversed. There He promised blessings only on condition of obedience and threatened curses if every part of it was not fulfilled. (See Deut. 28.) It is imperative that God's order under grace be not confused with that under law. It often is, because the order under law parallels the thinking of natural man. With the law God met man on man's own plane.

If it has pleased God to be careful to appeal for godly living because of His own work of grace, is it not incumbent upon believers to do likewise? Years of careful observation have revealed the common practice of using God's appeals, but entirely neglecting His work of grace as a basis for these appeals. How many urgent appeals have not been made using the partial text, "Present your bodies a living sacrifice, holy, acceptable unto God" (Rom. 12:1) without the slightest reference to the first part of the text, the real basis for the appeal, "I beseech you therefore, brethren, by the mercies of God." A clear presentation of the mercies of God as a basis for the appeal is rarely heard. Yet the Holy Spirit caused eight chapters to be devoted to telling of His mercies before He caused the appeal to be made. The same is true of all of God's appeals. This will be discussed more fully in a later chapter.

Most Christians consider God's appeals for a life pleasing unto Himself entirely apart from that particular work of grace to which He relates each appeal. May not this at least partly explain the present low spiritual level on which most believers live? God's appeals have no force when His arguments are ignored.

As God's arguments are omitted, it is natural that man's own arguments be substituted. Zeal and self-sacrifice of other Christians are used as an appeal. Touching stories of the need of the heathen are told. Their low moral, intellectual and temporal condition is vividly presented. "Your church" or "your denomination" needs your support is a common appeal. Even one's own self-respect is used as a reason for Christian service. The response, if any, easily becomes the fulfillment of a duty or the attainment to some great ideal and not a joyful and spontaneous labor of love for Christ.

As God's arguments for an appeal are disregarded, the "service" that follows is often done in dependence upon self instead of upon Him. When the appeal is based on God's work of grace the resultant conduct will be in dependence upon Him, and for His glory.

The eloquence and persuasive powers of a speaker or the enthusiasm of an occasion may move some people to action, but it will probably be lacking of depth and not be centered in God.

God's appeals for godly conduct are valid only when based on His own arguments. No one has a right to ask another to do what God asks and offer lesser arguments than does God. The things for which God appeals are so great, they cut so deeply into life, that nothing less than His own arguments justify compliance therewith. The fact that Adoniram Judson gave his life for Burma is no conclusive argument that anyone else must go; but the fact that Christ died for the Burmese, as well as for the one whom God calls, is an unanswerable argument for going, if God calls. The more that is made of the incarnation, death, resurrection, and intercessory work of Christ and of the fulness of God's work of grace, the stronger will be the appeal for godly living.

God's standards for life under grace are so high that it is impossible to appeal for them on the basis of human and moral thinking without detracting from their high requirements. God's own arguments are necessary to hold the appeals up to God's standards. Appeals based on human arguments necessarily lower the standards. By omitting God's arguments, standards for godly living are brought down from the divine plane to the level of human concepts.

Much exhortation is nothing more than a condemnation of vices. While it is often necessary to correct sins of believers this should always be related to God's work of grace for and in them. Vices should be shown as being of the old man and should be put off as being inconsistent with the believer's position before God. Condemnation of vices apart from God's work of grace tends to encourage a feeling of self-righteousness, a holier than thou attitude, in those who reform and in those who are not guilty; and a spirit of despair in those who repeatedly fail through personal weakness. Such condemnation emphasizes dependence upon self instead of dependence upon God.

Much prompting to godly living is purely negative. Participation in certain amusements and personal habits and manner of dress are condemned. At times this is done sensationally and unkindly. It becomes a matter of attacking this and forbidding that. Seldom is anything offered to replace that which is condemned. All of this produces a great void in life. As nature abhors a vacuum, so also does human life. There is a record of a life from which an unclean spirit had gone out, but returned, and finding the house swept and garnished but empty he brought seven others more wicked than himself and the last state of that man was worse than the first (Luke 11:25, 26).

While God is much concerned about keeping the lives of His people free from worldly things, His approach is far different from the above. God's way has been well stated in these words: "There are two methods that the Lord graciously adopts, to draw the heart away from the present world. The first is, by setting before it the attractiveness and stability of things above; the second is, by faithfully declaring the evanescent and shakable nature of things on the earth."

When the heart finds all its satisfaction in the things of God and in His Son, there is no need to condemn the transitory pleasures of the world. God offers far better things in the place of those which are to pass away. Much worldliness in the Church of Christ today is due to a failure to draw the hearts to Christ by teaching and emphasizing His attractiveness.

There is one more difference between the thoughts of God and the thoughts of man in relation to admonitions. God always bases His appeals upon some great fundamental principle, and relates individual acts thereto. Man usually deals with individual acts by themselves, apart from any basic principle. This is largely a legalistic point of view which considers specific offenses, and results in restrictive regulations with precept upon precept. Much of this type of thinking and teaching is being related to Christian conduct and appeals therefore. Is it any wonder that people, especially young people, have so many perplexing questions about so many details of life and so often say, May I do this, and must I refrain from that? Of this God says, "the letter killeth" (2 Cor. 3:6).

Paul, in dealing with the question of eating meat offered to idols, held that there was nothing wrong in so doing because the idol was nothing. But his own life was governed by the great principle; "Wherefore, if meat make my brother to offend, I will eat no flesh while the world standeth, lest I make my brother to offend." (1 Cor. 8:13).

There is unquestionably a place for instruction as to details of the conduct of a believer. Paul frequently mentioned specific things which should or should not be done. He calls upon the Corinthian Church to take part in a collection for the saints and relates it to the fact that their labor in the Lord shall not be in vain because of the certainty of the resurrection (Cor. 15 and 16:1). He urges putting away lying, anger, and stealing as a part of putting off of the old man and putting on of the new man, "which after God is created in righteousness and true holiness" (Eph. 4:17–29). How much more conclusive this than a mere condemnation of lying, anger and stealing.

To omit the basic principles upon which all admonitions of grace are based and to consider specific precepts by themselves is to miss the peculiar nature of grace teachings and to substitute ethical teachings in their place.

16

Some Promptings by Grace

THE apostolic writings abound in promptings to godly living based upon God's work of grace. Two of these are reserved for separate chapters. The following limited number are mentioned to illustrate the principle.

1. "Know ye not that your bodies are the members of Christ? shall I then take the members of Christ, and make them the members of a harlot? God forbid" (1 Cor. 6:15). In this appeal to flee fornication, a reminder is made of the fact that every believer is a member of the body of Christ. No mention is made of the immorality of the sin in question, nor the dishonor which comes upon one who practices it. Here is purely a question of the inconsistency of believers, who are members of the body of Christ, being brought into union with a harlot. Until believers are taught what it means to be a member of the body of Christ there is little if any appeal in this passage.

2. "What? know ye not that your body is the temple of the Holy Ghost which is in you, which ye have of God, and ye are not your own? For ye are bought with a price: therefore glorify God in your body, and in your spirit, which are God's" (1 Cor. 6:19, 20). This appeal is for a life to the glory of

God. It is based solely upon the two facts that the Holy Ghost indwells the believer and that Christ paid the price for his redemption. He is therefore not his own, he belongs to Christ. What stronger argument can there be for glorifying God in the body? How seldom these great cardinal truths are thought of as having any relationship whatsoever to the believer's conduct!

3. "And that he [Christ] died for all, that they which live should not henceforth live unto themselves, but unto him which died for them, and rose again" (2 Cor. 5:15). Christ died for all. He suffered the most painful death known, death on the cross. Even more, He suffered the indescribable agony of separation from God. "My God, my God, why hast thou forsaken me?" (Mark 15:34). His death for all was apart from any human merit, "while we were yet sinners, Christ died for us" (Rom. 5:8). This is God's reason why all who live (who have received life in Christ) should live, not unto themselves but unto Him, who died and rose again. It is unto a living Person; not unto a prophet whose body is rotting in some oriental grave. Nor is it according to a moral code or high ideals. To live unto self is to live for personal gain. To live unto Him is for His gain. To live unto Him is much more than to refrain from evil practices. It is placing His interests before one's own. It is doing things that please Him, not things that please self.

Grace teaches by emphasizing the great meaning of the death and resurrection of Christ and then appeals to those who have thereby received eternal life to live their earthly lives for Him. It must follow, then, that the more a believer sees in the death and resurrection of Jesus Christ, the more should his life be lived for Him. A life unto self, even though highly moral and cultured, is seen as inconsistent with the fact that Christ died and rose again. The realization of this great principle will resolve the multiplied questions as to conduct into one simple question; Is this living unto Him who died and rose again, or is it living unto self? To appeal for a life for Christ apart from this principle is to try to produce an effect without sufficient cause.

4. "Be ye not unequally yoked together with unbelievers: for what fellowship hath righteousness with unrighteousness? and what communion hath light with darkness? And what concord hath Christ with Belial? or what part hath he that believeth with an infidel? And what agreement hath the temple of God with idols? for ye are the temple of the living God; as God hath said, I will dwell in them, and walk in them; and I will be their God, and they shall be my people. Wherefore come out from among them, and be ye separate, saith the Lord, and touch not the unclean thing" (2 Cor. 6:14–17). The appeal to believers to be "not unequally yoked" with unbelievers is here based on the fact that the things which a believer is, by his position in Christ, are incompatible with those things which an unbeliever is because he is not in Christ, but in Belial. Because there is a clean cut

separation between things of God and the world, a believer should come out and be separate and not partake in unclean things. This does not mean asceticism for Paul elsewhere said, "I wrote unto you an espistle not to company with fornicators: Yet not altogether with the fornicators of the world, or with the covetous, or extortioners, or with idolaters; for them must ye needs go out of the world" (1 Cor. 5:9, 10).

5. Paul's appeal to the Corinthian saints to contribute to the poor at Jerusalem.is based on these words, "For ye know the grace of our Lord Jesus Christ, that though he was rich, yet for your sakes he became poor, that ye through.his poverty might be rich" (2 Cor. 8:9). How different from the many human arguments for sacrificial giving is not this reminder that Christ emptied Himself of His riches and glory in order that lost sinners might through Him become rich!

6. "If there be therefore any consolation in Christ, if any comfort of love, if any fellowship of the Spirit, if any bowels [compassions] and mercies, Fulfill ye my joy, that ye be likeminded, having the same love, being of one accord, of one mind. Let nothing be done through strife or vainglory; but in lowliness of mind let each esteem other better than themselves. Look not every man on his own things, but every man also on the things of others" (Phil. 2:1–4). The appeal to be likeminded, to live in love, to be of one accord, to let nothing be done in strife or vainglory, to esteem others better than one-

self, and to look not on one's own but also on the things of others is based on the fact that there is consolation in Christ, that there is in Him a comfort of love, a fellowship of the Spirit, and compassions and mercies.

7. "If ye then be risen with Christ, seek those things which are above, where Christ sitteth on the right hand of God. Set your affection on things above, not on things on the earth. For ye are dead, and your life is hid with Christ in God. When Christ, who is our life, shall appear, then shall ye also appear with him in glory" (Col. 3:1–4). Every believer is risen with Christ through faith (Col. 2:12). He has been taken out of this evil world of sin and spiritual death. He has been raised up together with Christ and made to sit in heavenly places in Him (Eph. 2:6). This is the most exalted position in God's entire economy. Should not one placed in this exalted position find his fullest enjoyment in the things that pertain thereto? The appeal is to set the affection on the things related to that position and not on the things belonging to the evil world from which one has been delivered. This appeal is not for deeds, but for a life filled with thoughts of the heavenly position; for a mind occupied with Christ and His glory, instead of the passing things of this world. The greatness of this position is emphasized by the declaration that the life is hid with Christ in God and when He, Christ, shall appear then shall all believers appear with Him in glory. It takes very little earthly glory to

captivate a human being. Why does not this high position, and this infinite glory, to be shared with Christ, captivate believers more, and result in seeking the things above? Is it because they are so seldom if ever told about it? Or is it because, in this rushing nervous age of action, few take time for meditation thereon? Surely God's method of teaching by grace cannot be wrong. Has the church of today failed to recognize this method?

8. These two great things, being risen with Christ and the certain future glory because the life is hid with Christ in God are made the reason for additional appeals. "Mortify [put to death] therefore your members which are upon the earth; fornication, uncleanness, inordinate affection, evil concupiscence, and covetousness, which is idolatry" (Col. 3:5). "But now ye also put off all these; anger, wrath, malice, blasphemy, filthy communication out of your mouth" (v. 8). "Put on therefore, as the elect of God, holy and beloved, bowels of mercies, kindness, humbleness of mind, meekness, longsuffering; Forbearing one another, and forgiving one another, if any man have a quarrel against any: even as Christ forgave you, so also do ye. And above all things put on charity, which is the bond of perfectness. And let the peace of God rule in your hearts" (vs. 12–15). "And whatsoever ye do in word or deed, do all in the name of the Lord Jesus, giving thanks to God and the Father by him" (v. 17). All of these ought to be done for the sole reason that the

believer is "risen with Christ" unto a newness of life.

9. "As ye know how we exhorted and comforted and charged everyone of you . . . That ye would walk worthy of God, who hath called you unto his kingdom and glory" (1 Thess. 2:11, 12). This calling is elsewher said to be "to the obtaining of the glory of our Lord Jesus Christ" (2 Thess. 2:14). No other creature of God has been called to the high and glorious position as are believers in the present age of grace. This is that which makes grace infinite. Can any denial of the pleasures of the world, or self-sacrifice, or unstinted giving out of one's self be too great in the light of this calling? And remember, this calling of God is without repentance (Rom. 11:29).

10. "Being born again, not of corruptible seed, but incorruptible, by the word of God, which liveth and abideth forever" (1 Pet. 1:23), is the reason given for laying aside all malice, and all guile, and hypocrisies, and envies, and all evil speakings, and as newborn babes, desire the sincere milk of the word (1 Pet. 2:1, 2).

11. "Beloved, now are we the sons [children] of God, and it doth not yet appear what we shall be: but we know that, when he shall appear, we shall be like him; for we shall see him as he is" (1 John 3:2). This is a plain, unconditional statement that all believers are now the children of God and when Christ shall appear, all shall be changed into the

very likeness of Him. The anticipation of this great transformation into the very likeness of Christ calls for a life on earth that partakes of His purity. "And every man that hath this hope in him purifieth himself, even as he is pure" (v. 3).

The things on which the above appeals, and many others, are based are spoken of as fully accomplished. Nothing can be added to them. There is no uncertainty about them. They are established and unalterable facts. All belong to God's work of grace, and have been brought about by Him. They are not conditioned upon any human merit nor action. All are divine values. Not one is on a purely moral or human level. How convincing, how conclusive, and how different these are from man's impotant arguments for Christian conduct!

Present day neglect and ignorance of God's work of grace and His appeals based thereon are appalling. One of the greatest needs of the day is a clear and faithful presentation of God's work of grace on behalf of the believer and when that has been done, an appeal for conduct on a high spiritual level in harmony therewith.

17

Present Your Bodies

I BESEECH you therefore, brethren, by the mercies of God, that ye present your bodies a living sacrifice, holy, acceptable unto God, which is your reasonable service. And be not conformed to this world: but be ye transformed by the renewing of your mind, that ye may prove what is that good, and acceptable, and perfect, will of God" (Rom. 12:1, 2).

This passage contains probably the strongest appeal in the Scriptures for a complete surrender to God. It involves the mind as well as the body. The plea is that the body be made a living sacrifice. The word sacrifice signifies a change of ownership for the purpose of being consumed, and that for the benefit of the new owner. A sacrifice is presented by man to God and is something that has real value to the one who offers it. In the Old Testament that which was sacrificed to God had to be perfect: anything with a blemish or any defect whatsoever was not acceptable unto Him. The sacrifice here in question is to be a living one. This can only mean that the sacrifice of the believer's body is to be continuous and one that brings forth results. Paul said, "I am offered daily." It is also to be holy and acceptable unto God. This is only possible when the body is pure and undefiled by sin.

119

This sacrifice is called "your reasonable service." To give one's body entirely to God, to be burned out in service for Him; to deny oneself all things that are pleasant to man for His sake seems to man a most unreasonable thing. Why should anyone give up all that is pleasing in this world if God so wills and live solely to please Him?

In addition to the sacrifice of the body, the entire being should be transformed by the renewing of the mind so as not to be conformed to this world, but to the "good, and acceptable, and perfect will of God." The renewing of the mind has to do with the intellect. It is not the emotions that are here considered. The intellect is more stable than the emotions, or the feelings. While it is not denied that there is place in the Christian life for feelings, there is need for a real intellectual transformation. Too many appeals are addressed to the emotions and have little lasting value.

That which Paul here urges is vastly more than living on a high moral plane, and the self-sacrifice called for can never be made to seem reasonable on the basis of any human arguments. Yet it is called a reasonable service. What then makes it reasonable? The whole issue rests on the introductory words, "I beseech you therefore, brethren, by the mercies of God." It is only beause of the mercies of God that it is reasonable for those called brethren to comply with this exhortation. This being true, it is essential for one who is to make such a sacrifice to understand these mercies of God. The word "therefore" shows that Paul rests the whole argument on that which he has in the preceding chapters taught about these mercies.

As Paul pleaded on the basis of "the mercies of God," it is perfectly clear that his appeal is without force until these mercies are known, understood, and accepted. The more clearly they are understood the greater is the force of the argument. On the other hand, if the study of these mercies of God is neglected the force of the appeal is lost, and there is no reason for heeding it. It thus becomes evident that neglect of the study and the teaching of the doctrines of the grace of God, can lead to nothing else than failure in godly living. To omit a presentation of God's mercies as a basis for this appeal is to entirely void the appeal. But that very thing is usually done when this passage is used as an appeal for a sacrificial life.

Grace, then, here as always, first lays a foundation for its appeal by setting forth the things which God has done for the believer, and then, with that as a basis, makes the appeal for conduct which is reasonable only in view of that which God has done.

Space permits but a brief reference to these mercies of God on which the appeal is based.

The first part of Romans (1:18 to 3:20) deals with the sinfulness of man and concludes that "There is none righteous, no, not one; . . . there is none that seeketh after God, . . . there is none that doeth good, no, not one" (3:10–12). Man is shown to be incapable of doing anything whatsoever that is acceptable to God. Being guilty before Him, man is subject to everlasting condemnation.

But a righteousness of God has been manifested by Jesus Christ. This righteousness is offered to all men, even to those of whom it was said, "there is none righteous." Moreover, it is upon all who believe in Jesus Christ. By this he who receives Jesus Christ becomes, in the sight of God, even as righteous as is Christ. In other words, he is justified. All of this has been made possible by the redemption that is in Christ Jesus, because He on the Cross satisfied the demands of God's justice. God is therefore free to count everyone righteous who believes in Jesus Christ. All of this has been accomplished by God for man, apart from any human merits (3:21–27).

Special emphasis is placed on the fact that man cannot work for his justification. It is the one who believes in Christ that is counted righteous and this is solely because of his faith (Chapter 4).

He who is justified has peace with God and has access by faith into the grace wherein he stands (5:2). In other words, God will always respond to his faith with further manifestations of His grace.

God does not only justify one who believes, He has made a provision to save from His wrath everyone who is justified. "But God commendeth his love toward us, in that, while we were yet sinners, Christ died for us. Much more then, being now justified by his blood, we shall be saved from wrath through him" (5:8, 9). If it were not for this mercy of God, the believer's body and mind would forever be subject to the torment of the wrath of God. But according to this statement, it is "much more" to God that the believer be saved from His wrath than the already certain fact that he has been justified. It is that body which is saved from wrath that God asks to have presented unto Himself. It is that mind which but for this mercy would throughout all eternity be conscious of its lost estate, He wants renewed, so that during this brief span of life it will be in conformity to His will. Is not that most reasonable?

"For if, when we were enemies, we were reconciled to God by the death of his Son, much more, being reconciled, we shall be saved by his life" (5:10). There was a time when we were enemies, that is rebels, to God. The penalty for rebellion is death, but His Son, in a human body, died, and paid the penalty for that rebellion. Thereby we have been reconciled to God. We are no more at enmity to Him. Jesus Christ is now living for the express purpose of keeping us saved. Here again is a mercy by which God pleads for a surrendered life, a life lived for Him. And why should it not be so? Jesus Christ gave His *body* in suffering and death to bring us to God. In His resurrected *body* He is living in Heaven on our behalf. It truly is a reasonable service to present to God as a living sacrifice the *body* that has been so reconciled and is being so kept by Him. And the mind, which was reconciled at so great a cost ought surely be renewed so that it may know and be conformed to the good and perfect and acceptable will of God.

"But if the spirit of Him that raised up Jesus from the dead dwell in you, he that raised up Christ from the dead shall also quicken your mortal bodies by his Spirit that dwelleth in you" (8:11). "For I reckon that the sufferings of this present time are not worthy to be compared with the glory which shall be revealed in us" (v. 18). "For whom he did foreknow, he also did predestinate to be conformed to the image of his Son" (v. 29). This conformity to the Son of God is elsewhere explained by Paul, "we look for the Saviour, the Lord Jesus Christ: Who shall change our vile body, that it may be fashioned like unto his glorious body" (Phil. 3:20, 21). In these verses is seen a mercy of God so great that it cannot be fully fathomed by the finite human mind. The present mortal bodies of believers, subject to death and corruption, shall be raised from death and made like unto the glorious body of the Son of God. That surely is a glory with which the sufferings of the present time are not worthy to be compared. In view of this mercy of God it is reasonable to present to Him for His use, that body which is to be so glorified, even though it does mean suffering for a while.

"For I am persuaded, that neither death, nor life, nor angels, nor principalities, nor powers, nor things present, nor things to come, Nor height, nor depth, nor any other creature, shall be able to separate us from the love of God, which is in Christ

Jesus our Lord" (Rom. 8:38, 39). This mercy is the climax of all, and is all-inclusive, for grace is God's love in action, and if nothing can separate the believer from the love of God which is in Christ Jesus, then the believer is assured that God's grace will, for time and eternity, operate in his behalf. It is this unfailing love, this unending love, to which God points in appealing for a mind that is conformed to His good, and acceptable and perfect will.

These are some of the great mercies of God to which Paul refers when he says, "Therefore, brethren, I beseech you by the mercies of God." These mercies are altogether sufficient reason for a believer to present his body unto God as a living sacrifice and to conform his own will to the good and perfect will of God. No human appeal, no sacrifice made by other Christians, no question of self-respect, no moral issues, nor any emotional appeal will have the weight which these mercies of God have.

18

Walk Worthy of Your Calling

I THEREFORE, the prisoner of the Lord, beseech you that ye walk worthy of the vocation [calling] wherewith ye are called" (Eph. 4:1). This appeal is for an earthly life in full harmony with the exalted position to which the believer has been called. The introductory word "therefore" points back to certain things presented in the preceding chapters which are the basis for the appeal. In those chapters is found the greatest revelation of the present position and eternal destiny of all who believe.

The appeal is not to live so as to gain the high calling. That is impossible, for the position is so high that it cannot possibly be earned, not even by a perfect life, if that were possible. The position belongs to the believer and is his because of God's calling and His own purpose, and is a gift of His grace. As the calling is unalterable (Rom. 11:29), this appeal can never lose its force.

Children born into a royal family are taught to conduct themselves as becomes royalty because they are that by birth. They honor the king and their country only as they so conduct themselves. They are forbidden many things which other children may do. The street waif of the lower East Side of

New York cannot be urged to live as a prince. He does not hold that position. The royal position is the basis for the appeal for royal conduct. So when Paul wrote "I therefore," he pointed to the believer's high and exalted calling as the reason, in fact the only reason, for a life in harmony therewith. This calling is sufficient reason for the appeal. When understood, it completely eliminates many whys and wherefores as to Christian conduct. A clear understanding and acceptance of all that is included in the believer's calling are therefore essential as the background for a godly life. What then is this calling?

The long list of things which make up the believer's calling is introduced by the words, "Blessed be the God and Father of our Lord Jesus Christ, who hath blessed us with all spiritual blessings in heavenly places in Christ" (Eph. 1:3). This at once identifies the calling as spiritual and related to heavenly things. The walk to be worthy must, then, be of a spiritual order, on a heavenly plane. This is more than a fine moral life.

"He [God] hath chosen us in him [Christ] before the foundation of the world, that we should be holy and without blame before him in love" (v. 4). This is nothing less than eternal enjoyment of God's limitless love. This position, in His presence, is that of a son, for God has "predestinated us unto the adoption of children [sons] by Jesus Christ to himself, according to the good pleasure of his will" (v. 5). God has Himself determined, according to the good pleasure of His will, that in the eternal state all believers shall be His sons. This is a family relationship, a position higher than that of any other celestial being. All this is because the believer is accepted of God in His beloved Son (v. 6). It is as when a son brings home a bride; though previously an entire stranger, she is accepted into the family because of her union with the son.

In the beloved Son, the believer also has redemption through His blood, and forgiveness of sins according to the riches of the infinite grace of God (v. 7), and in addition an inheritance purposed by God Himself after the counsel of His own will (v. 11). The Holy Spirit has been given as a seal for this and as an earnest that the inheritance shall be received (v. 14).

Then is told why and how God has done all this. "But God, who is rich in mercy, for his great love wherewith he loved us, Even when we were dead in sins, hath quickened us together with Christ, (by grace ye are saved;) And hath raised us up together, and made us sit together in heavenly places in Christ Jesus" (Eph. 2:4–6). God has done all purely because of His mercy and great love. No human merit entered here, it was "when we were [spiritually] dead in trespasses and sins." Even more, He has "made us sit together in heavenly places in Christ Jesus"; the very place where God set Christ when He raised Him from the dead. This position is "Far above all principality, and power, and might, and dominion, and every name that is named, not only in this world, but also in that which is to come" (Eph. 1:20, 21). Here again is emphasis on the exalted position of the believer.

God's purpose in all is, "That in the ages to come he might show the exceeding riches of his grace in his kindness toward us through Christ Jesus" (2:7). Think of it! Throughout all eternity to be the object of the exceeding riches of God's grace. What an eternity! What a position! What a calling! It is infinite in its glory, and infinite in its duration.

In contrast to this unspeakably high and glorious position, believers are reminded that in the time past they "were without Christ, being aliens . . . and strangers . . . having no hope, and without God in the world" (v. 12). But now in Christ Jesus they are made high by the blood of Christ (v. 13). They are therefore now "no more strangers and foreigners, but fellow citizens with the saints, and of the household of God" (v. 19). And in the Lord they "are builded together for an habitation of God through the Spirit" (v. 22).

All of the above is descriptive of the calling of God of which every believer should walk worthy. It has been asked, "Does your life square with your profession?" There is a more fundamental question: Is your life worthy of your position? That is the only true measure for the believer's life.

It is only after having set forth this exalted position and because of it that the appeal is made for a worthy walk. The first condition of such a walk is not expressed in action, nor deeds, but is a state of mind and heart. It should be "With all lowliness and meekness, with longsuffering, forbearing one another in love; Endeavoring to keep the unity of the Spirit in the bond of peace" (4:2, 3). These are not characteristics of natural man, but of the life that is worthy of the high calling in Christ.

To cause a believer to see, with Paul, that "By the grace of God I am what I am" and that the glorious calling of God is all of grace and in no way of one's self, is God's way of teaching lowliness, meekness, longsuffering, forbearance, and unity of the spirit.

Another condition of the life worthy of the high calling of God, is growth and development of the spiritual life. Grace has made special provision for this in giving apostles, prophets, evangelists, pastors and teachers; "For the perfecting of the saints, . . . for the edifying of the body of Christ: Till we all come in the unity of the faith, and of the knowledge of the Son of God, unto a perfect man, unto the measure of the stature of the fulness of Christ: That we henceforth be no more children, tossed to and fro, and carried about with every wind of doctrine, by the sleight of men, and cunning craftiness" (4:7, 11–14). Because of this provision for spiritual growth and development, to remain immature and lacking in the knowledge of the things of Christ is to walk unworthy of the calling.

It was only after having discussed the state of mind and heart above that Paul referred to specific acts of conduct. Even then he did so by relating these acts to putting off of the things of the "old man" and putting on the things of the "new man." The "old man" is the natural unregenerated man. His walk is in the vanity of his own mind. His understanding is darkened as to the divine spiritual values. Through ignorance thereof he is alienated from the life of God. He is spiritually corrupt by deceitful lusts (vs. 17, 18, 22). The new man knows Christ and "after God is created in righteousness and true holiness" (vs. 20, 24). The test, therefore, of individual acts is whether they are things that belong to the old or to the new man. If the former they should be put off. But for each act of the old man that is put off there is a corresponding act of the new man to be put on. The walk is not made worthy of the calling by merely putting off the things of the old man: the things of the new man must also be put on. The worthy walk is not negative, it is definitely positive.

The teaching concerning putting off things of the old man, and putting on those of the new is one of the most important of all grace teachings. It does seem reasonable that one who has been taken out of the world, and translated into the kingdom of the Son of God should no longer live as does the world, but as a new being. If Christians had a basic understanding of the nature of the old man and of the new and of the things belonging to each, they would see the inconsistency of continuing in the old. Not

until Christian conduct is related to the high calling in Christ Jesus, can there be a clear understanding as to the why, or why not, of many things.

Only after the contrast between the old man and
the new have been set forth are admonitions made
concerning specific acts. "Wherefore putting away
lying, speak every man truth with his neighbour"
(v. 25). "Let him that stole steal no more: but rather
let him labour, working with his hands the thing
which is good, that he may have to give to him that
needeth" (v. 28). "Let no corrupt communication
proceed out of your mouth, but that which is good
to the use of edifying, that it may minister grace
unto the hearers" (v. 29). "Let all bitterness, and
wrath, and anger, and clamour, and evil speaking,
be put away from you, with all malice: And be ye
kind one to another, tenderhearted, forgiving one
another" (vs. 31, 32). All above negative qualities
are to be put off, being of the old man, and the
positive put on as being of the new man.

Another characteristic of the walk worthy of the
calling is to be "followers of God, as dear children,"
walking in love (5:1,2). Believers should also refrain
from things that belong to darkness, and should live
as children of light, which they are by their calling
(v. 8).

"And be not drunk with wine, wherein is excess;
but be filled with the Spirit" (v. 18) is another essential of the walk that is worthy of the calling. He
who is so filled with the Spirit will live a joyous
life, "Giving thanks always for all things unto God

the Father in the name of our Lord Jesus Christ"
(v. 20).

Relationships with other persons, to be worthy
of the calling, should be as though they actually
were between the believer and his Lord. Wives are
asked to submit themselves to their husbands as
unto the Lord (v. 22). Husbands should love their
wives as Christ has loved the church and given Himself for it (v. 25). Servants, or slaves as they then
were, should serve their masters "With good will
doing service, as to the Lord, and not to men"; and
masters should do the same to their servants (6:7, 9).

Finally, the worthy walk is said to be a conflict
with Satan and the evil spiritual forces of darkness
of this world. For this conflict the believer must be
girt about with truth, have the breastplate of righteousness, the feet shod with the preparation of the
gospel of peace, the shield of faith, the helmet of
salvation, and the sword of the Spirit, which is the
word of God (6:12–17).

The admonition closes with the words, "Praying
always with all prayer and supplication in the Spirit,
and watching thereunto with all perseverance and
supplication for all saints" (v. 18).

All of the above are essential to a life worthy of
the high calling of God in Christ. This life is on an
infinitely higher plane than that governed by merely
moral standards. It is life on a divine plane lived on
earth. Only the calling is sufficient argument for the
admonition.

19

Chastening

ONE aspect of the discipline by grace is not always recognized as being of grace. It is the chastening of the Lord. The finest passage on this subject is Hebrews 12:5-11. "And ye have forgotten the exhortation that speaketh unto you as unto children, My son, despise not thou the chastening of the Lord, nor faint when thou art rebuked of him: For whom the Lord loveth he chasteneth, and scourgeth every son whom he receiveth. If ye endure chastening, God dealeth with you as with Sons; for what son is he whom the father chasteneth not? But if ye be without chastisement [chastening R.V.], whereof all are partakers, then are ye bastards, and not sons. Furthermore we have had fathers of our flesh which corrected us, and we gave them reverence: shall we not much rather be in subjection unto the Father of spirits, and live? For they verily for a few days chastened us after their own pleasure; but he for our profit, that we might be partakers of his holiness. Now no chastening for the present seemeth to be joyous, but grievous; nevertheless afterward it yieldeth the peaceable fruit of righteousness unto them which are exercised thereby."

Chastening is God the Father dealing with His child in love. "For whom the Lord loveth he chas-

teneth, and scourgeth every son whom he receiveth."
It is a sign of sonship and a reminder that one has
not been forsaken by God.

Because chastening is at times accompanied by
the visitation of distress and affliction, it is often
confused with punishment. This is not true, for
punishment is God the judge, in justice, exacting
the full penalty of His broken law. Here is no father-
hood of God and no expression of His love. Punishment is the wrath of God poured out upon all who
reject His Son. It is condemnation that shall come
upon the unbelieving world. The believer in Jesus
Christ "shall not come into condemnation; but is
passed from death unto life" (John 5:24). He is not
under law but under grace (Rom. 6:14).

Let no one presume upon the grace of God and
think that because he shall not come into condemnation (that is, be lost) he can live according to the
desires of his old carnal nature without suffering the
full consequences thereof. God does deal with the
sins of believers. This is by chastening and is described by no milder term than scourging. No believer should overlook the warning, "For our God
is a consuming fire" (Heb. 12:29). He shall surely
burn out everything that is unpleasing to Him.

God's chastening is to correct and to purify. It
implies imperfection but not guilt. Gold is chastened that it may become pure. Intense heat melts
it into a liquid and thus separates from it all impurities. The dew drop sparkling in the early morn-
ing was by the heat of yesterday's sun drawn as

vapor from the stagnant pool. The cool of the night condensed it into water so pure that it refracts the rays of the sun into the full beauty of the spectrum. Both of these processes are for the sole purpose of purification. So also is the chastening by the Father's love. It is to remove all which is unpleasing to Him.

This answers the question, Why do the righteous suffer? The unrighteous (all who have not accepted the righteousness of God which is Christ) are not, in the sight of God, gold to be chastened. There is no spiritual life to free from the impurities of the world. They are dead in trespasses and sins (Eph. 2:1). While the unrighteous do not now suffer by chastening there awaits them judgment and fiery indignation, which shall devour them (Heb. 10:27), unless they by faith receive Jesus Christ.

What then are the impurities to be removed by chastening? As the purpose of the discipline by grace is to produce godly living (and this was seen to be complete dependence upon God), it follows that all in the life of a believer that is not in dependence upon Him is an impurity. Every self-centered thing is included; all dependence upon self, all self-will, all satisfaction of selfish desires, and all glory for self. Many humanly admirable things together with all worldly desires and all immorality require the chastening work of God.

At times chastening is a preventive work. Paul experienced such chastening. These are his own words describing it, "And lest I should be exalted above measure through the abundance of the revelations, there was given to me a thorn in the flesh, the messenger of Satan to buffet me, lest I should be exalted above measure" (2 Cor. 12:7). This provision of God's grace was a means to hold in subjection the tendency of the flesh to boast. How necessary that is!

The one purpose of this purifying work of the Father is that we might be partakers of His holiness. "For God hath not called us unto uncleanness, but unto holiness" (1 Thess. 4:7). The second purpose is that it might yield "the peaceable fruit of righteousness unto them which are exercised thereby" (vs. 10, 11). Holiness connotes spiritual purity or freedom from sinful affections, in fact, all that is in any way contrary to God's holiness. Righteousness means unswerving rectitude and life to the divine will. Holiness is a state of being: righteousness is the expression of that state.

The peaceable fruit of righteousness is said to be unto them which are exercised by the chastening. This implies possibility of resisting the chastening of the Father. The clay must yield to the potter's "exercise" if it is to become a vessel of beauty. The gold must yield to the "exercise" of the fire to become pure. The drop of water must yield to the "exercise" of the sun's rays and the cool of the night to be transformed into the dew drop. "Yield" is the key word in each case. So the believer is exercised by the chastening only as he yields to the hand of God.

It should be recognized that this fruit of righteousness is *unto* not *by* them that are exercised. It is produced by God in their lives. This fruit is peaceable. Peace comes with the chastening of the Lord to those who are exercised thereby. It is a rest in His wisdom to do all things well.

But some are not exercised by the chastening. They pass through the trials that God sends and come out without yielding to God's hand. These the Lord shall deal with in His own way after this life has been passed. The unmistakable teaching concerning this is, "Now if any man build upon this foundation [Jesus Christ] gold, silver, precious [costly R.V.] stones, wood, hay, stubble; Every man's work shall be made manifest: for the day shall declare it, because it shall be revealed by fire; and the fire shall try every man's work of what sort it is. If any man's work abide which he hath built thereupon, he shall receive a reward. If any man's work shall be burned, he shall suffer loss: but he himself shall be saved; yet so as by fire" (1 Cor. 3:12–15).

That the issue here is not the question of eternal life or everlasting damnation is clear from the words "but he himself shall be saved," which are said of the one who suffers loss. That it refers to believers and not to unsaved is clear from the fact that building is upon the foundation Jesus Christ.

Two groups of three words each, describe the different materials with which a believer builds. In the one group are things which stand the test of fire; the other, things that are consumed thereby.

Wood, hay, and stubble, used figuratively, speak

of humanity and the things of the flesh. Wood is a more valuable building material than hay. It can be shaped and beautifully finished and has a certain degree of durability and stability. Hay lacks both these qualities. Stubble is always spoken of as only being fit for burning. All these represent human accomplishments; things done in self-will, by human power, for self-gratification, and for acceptance by men. To men some seem very attractive and enduring; others have little or no value and are transitory. To God all are the same, without value, only to be consumed by His fire.

Gold, silver and costly stones stand the test of fire and endure. Gold, in the Bible, symbolizes deity, the things of God. Silver symbolizes redemption through Jesus Christ. The costly stones must refer to valuable building stones, as the enduring granite, used for structures of great and lasting value. Believers are called "living stones" built into a spiritual house (1 Pet. 2:5 R.V.) of which Christ is the cornerstone.

This points to the thought that only those works which are of God, according to His will and by His power; those which further the redemptive work of Christ; and those which in some way contribute to the building of the church of Christ will survive God's test by fire.

It is a most sobering thought that the consuming fire of God shall burn out everything that does not contribute to God's purpose for this age. For many believers, this may be all their earthly life. The righteous man Lot (2 Pet. 2:8) was pushed out of Sodom just before it and all that he had accomplished while there were destroyed. Lot himself was saved, yet so as by fire. How many believers are not like Lot?

But those whose building abides shall receive a reward. It is, however, of great importance to recognize that the reward is not given because of the amount of building that has been done but because of the kind of materials used. These materials must be in accordance with God's plan for the building. A great amount of building with wood, hay and stubble will produce a large fire. A small amount of building with gold, silver and costly stones will endure and be rewarded. What a disillusionment it will be for large numbers of extremely active believers to find that they shall suffer a great loss instead of receiving a great reward.

It is popularly thought that much and faithful service for Christ will earn for a believer a better position in heaven. In other words, a personal gain will accrue to one who does much for God. This emphasis is entirely out of harmony with God's plan of grace, because it makes self-gain the object of the endeavor. When this happens the motive is no longer love, and that which is done is not a labor of love for Christ.

Rewards cannot be the payment of a debt owed by God to one who has done much for Him, for that would violate the basic principle of grace that God gives everything freely out of His Own loving heart. Nothing in the eternal state will have been earned by the efforts of those who by grace and grace alone have been granted access thereto. Rewards will be the gift of God's grace just as truly as is the gift of eternal life.

To make personal gain the motive for endeavor also violates Paul's admonition, "Whatsoever ye do, do all to the glory of God." Even the rewards, or crowns as they are called, shall be a means by which Christ shall be glorified, for the saints shall cast their crowns before His throne saying, "Thou art worthy, O Lord, to receive glory and honour and power: for thou hast created all things, and for thy pleasure they are and were created" (Rev. 4:11).

Rewards, then, are not to be thought of as being personal gain, but as an incentive to live pleasing unto God, as an indication of His approval of one's life, and as an additional means of glorifying Christ.

He who builds with gold, silver and costly stones uses the things that are of God. He builds in full dependence upon Him, both His power and His will. The love of Christ, not the expectation of reward, constrains him to build. He is concerned, not with personal glory, but that God be given all the glory. This kind of building and only this, God, through the operation of His infinite grace, rewards. All else shall burn. It is well to again be reminded that "Our God is a consuming fire."

20

Christk Pre-eminent

THE work of the Holy Spirit is to glorify Christ. Jesus said of Him, "He shall glorify me: for he shall receive of mine, and shall shew it unto you" (John 16:14). If the work of the Holy Spirit is to magnify Christ, it follows that it is God's purpose that the believer shall see the fullness of beauty in Him. When the mind and heart thus become occupied with Christ, the grace and truth of which He is full must become a great influence for godly living. On the contrary, when a believer struggles in self-effort to do that which he thinks right, the mind becomes occupied with self and the soul is drawn away from Christ. Therefore when the Holy Spirit takes of the things that are Christ's and shows them to the believer He is carrying out God's purpose of teaching by grace.

It was by presenting gifts from Isaac and telling about him that Abraham's servant attracted the heart of Rebecca so that she left her home and family and went with him to become Isaac's bride. So also the Holy Spirit by glorifying Christ seeks to draw believers away from the things of the world and bring them to Christ. The Holy Spirit never leads anyone to look at himself and his own accomplishments, but only and always at Christ and His work.

Paul expressed to the believers at Ephesus his desire and prayer on their behalf in these words, "That Christ might dwell in your hearts by faith; that ye, being rooted and grounded in love, may be able to comprehend with all saints what is the breadth, and length, and depth, and height; And to know the love of Christ, which passeth knowledge, that ye might be filled with all the fulness of God" (Eph. 3:17–19). Here is emphasis on a Person and His love. It is not a matter of fulfilling commandments or obligations, not duties to perform, nor even of living up to high ideals and moral standards. Paul's desire was that Christ might dwell in their hearts. The heart is the seat of the emotions which stir one's whole being. This is something in addition to an intellectual knowledge of Him, as important as that is. It is a realization of Him as the controlling force of one's own life. It is a consciousness of oneness with Him. The closest thing in human experience to this is that place which a man or woman has in the heart of the other, when they have become true lovers. Then each dwells in the heart of the other by faith. All of the thoughts and acts of the young man are influenced by "her" and have the one end in view of being pleasing to "her" and bringing "her" happiness. On her side, life becomes so occupied with "him" that to please "him" becomes her first desire. The life of neither is full apart from the other. Neither thinks of self apart from the other, and each gives the other the pre-eminence.

When Christ dwells in the heart of the believer by faith, life with all its acts and emotions, becomes centered in Him. That is why the Holy Spirit in this age takes the things that are of Christ and makes them known to those who are His. He glorifies Christ so that He may become pre-eminent in the life of the believer.

Paul, expressing his desire for himself, said, "But what things were gain to me, those I counted loss for Christ. Yea doubtless, and I count all things but loss for the excellency of the knowledge of Christ Jesus my Lord: for whom I have suffered the loss of all things, and do count them but dung, that I may win Christ, . . . That I may know him" (Phil. 3:7, 8, 10). It was not immoral things that Paul counted for loss and that were put away; nor were they questionable things or forbidden by law. It was highly respectable things which had been of great value to him. And why did he give up these things? Not because he did not have a right to enjoy them, but for the sole reason that he might win Christ, not as his Saviour, but as his ALL. One infinitely greater and more precious than everything in the world had captivated the soul of Paul.

To please his Lord was Paul's greatest desire. It completely possessed his entire being. His whole life was directly related to Christ. He said, "For me to live is Christ, and to die is gain" (Phil. 1:21). It cannot be a mere coincidence that to Paul, more than to any other man, God had revealed the exceeding riches of His grace, and that it was first given to him to preach the unsearchable riches of Christ. In the life of Paul is seen, as in no other person, the fullest effect of the grace of God.

Beholding Christ and His glory transforms the life of a believer. "But we all, with open face beholding as in a glass the glory of the Lord, are changed into the same image from glory to glory, even as by the Spirit of the Lord" (2 Cor. 3:18). This does not refer to that transformation which shall take place as believers behold Christ when He appears to receive His Own unto Himself. It refers to a possibility in the present life, even in anticipation of that great event. To be occupied with self, with one's own interests, with endless questionings as to what may and may not be done, brings distress and enslaves the soul. To behold Christ, and be occupied with Him and His beauty and grace produces liberty and conformity to His image. Someone has said, "To be occupied with self is despair: to be occupied with Christ is glory."

It is God's purpose concerning His Son "that in all things he might have the pre-eminence" (Col. 1:18). "For of him, and through him, and to him, are all things" (Rom. 11:36). "For by him were all things created, that are in heaven, and that are in earth, visible and invisible, whether they be thrones, or dominions, or principalities, or powers: all things were created by him, and for him" (Col. 1:16, 17). "In whom are hid all the treasures of wisdom and knowledge" (Col. 2:3). "For in him dwelleth all the fulness of the Godhead bodily" (Col. 2:9). He is seated "Far above all principality, and power, and might, and dominion, and every name that is named, not only in this world, but also in that which is to come" (Eph. 1:21).

It has previously been seen that grace points to things that God has freely done and bids the believer to live worthy thereof. But grace does even more, it points to Christ by whom all these blessings come and magnifies Him and seeks devotion to Him. This is vastly more than devotion to a cause, or a movement or an organization. It is devotion to a Person and that Person has of God been made pre-eminent over ALL things. Grace strives to make Him pre-eminent in the believer's life.

When Christ replaces everything else, even self, as the center of life, the things of the world lose their attractiveness and eternal things take on new value. Then there remains but one question in relation to conduct: Is Christ pleased with this? is He magnified by it? This will be true even though it means the loss of the earthly life. The greatest desire of the apostle Paul was that always "Christ shall be magnified in my body, whether it be by life, or by death" (Phil. 1:20). It was the gospel of the grace of God that had so transformed him.

How important is it not, then, to always present the pre-eminent Christ; to tell of His dying love for sinners, His present care for his own, and their future glory in union with Him—in fact, all that is included in the one word GRACE. This is grace "teaching us" to keep the eyes fixed upon Christ, and thereby draw them from the things of the world, yes even the finer things of the world, the high moral things, the cultural things, not to mention the questionable things. These worldly things will lose their value when the heart sees Christ in all His grace and glory.

21

Looking for His Appearing

THUS far the discussion of the teaching by grace
has been concerned with the present; with denying ungodliness and worldly lusts, and living soberly, righteously and godly in the present world.
Grace also teaches to look to the future—to look for
"that blessed hope, and the glorious appearing of
the great God and our Saviour Jesus Christ." The
emphasis here is not so much on His coming as on
the fact that the believer should be looking for that
event. He should be in a state of constant expectancy
of His Lord's return. This state of expectancy will
exert an important influence upon the believer's
life. That is why grace teaches believers to look for
the blessed hope.

The appearing of the Lord Jesus Christ in the
clouds to receive His own, His Church, unto Himself is the greatest vision that God has given to any
people. This event will usher in the eternal state
for everyone who in the present age has believed in
Jesus Christ. For all who have died in Christ it shall
mean the reuniting of the spirit with the body.
Then shall the corruptible bodies be changed into
incorruption, and the mortal shall take on immortality (1 Cor. 15:53). Then shall they be conformed
to the image of the Son of God (Rom. 8:29). They

shall be clothed in bodies fashioned like unto the glorious body of Jesus Christ (Phil. 3:21).

This coming for His own must not be confused with Christ's coming to set up His kingdom and rule in righteousness over all the earth as foretold by the Old Testament prophets. When these two events are confused with each other the teachings of grace are largely lost. The first event has to do with a heavenly position for every believer; the second, with earthly blessings, primarily for Israel but also through them to the nations of the earth.

Vision plays a great role in the lives of men. A vision will keep a man in a straight course until it is realized. It will bear him up during days of severe trial and hardships. It will cause him to deny himself things which might interfere with the fullest accomplishment of his vision. A vision is a great disciplinarian. It is a true teacher. A vision is one of the greatest formative influences in the life of any individual or group of people. Vision is so important that it was said of old, "Where there is no vision, the people perish." It is because of this power of a vision to transform the very life of a person that grace teaches the believer to look for the appearing of the Lord Jesus Christ. This being true it is hardly to be expected that the proper outlook upon life will be found among believers who do not look for this great event and are not aware of its importance to them. It is unthinkable that when this truth has gripped a person it will not leave a deep and lasting impression on his life.

Jesus, personally, first announced that He would return to receive His own unto Himself. He said, "Let not your heart be troubled: . . . In my Father's house are many mansions: if it were not so, I would have told you. I go to prepare a place for you. And if I go and prepare a place for you, I will come again, and receive you unto myself; that where I am, there ye may be also" (John 14:1–3).

It is important to notice that Jesus in making this initial announcement of His return, began by saying, "Let not your heart be troubled." The disciples were about to pass through the most discouraging period of their lives. Their Master, whom they had followed for three years, and who was everything to them, was about to be taken from them. That, if anything, was ample cause for troubled hearts. It was in view of this, that Jesus promised to return and receive them unto Himself. He gave them a vision of an eternity in fellowship with Himself. What if they had to face sorrows, disappointments, losses, and discouragements for a while? That was but for a moment compared to eternity with Him in the many dwelling places which He went to prepare.

Paul, after describing the Lord's return, closed with these words, "so shall we ever be with the Lord." Then he added, "Wherefore comfort one another with these words" (1 Thess. 4:15–18). Nothing can produce an untroubled heart in a world of turmoil as can the promise of the Lord's return. The most punctilious law observance or following the highest moral teachings will not do it. It is grace teaching the believer to look for the Lord's coming to receive him unto Himself that makes it possible to pass through the trials, testings and losses of this world with an untroubled heart.

Constant anticipation of the appearing of the Lord and of the glorious eternal existence in union with Him enabled Paul to bear suffering. He said, "For I reckon that the sufferings of this present time are not worthy to be compared with the glory which shall be revealed in us" (Rom. 8:18).

Purity of life is another effect produced in a believer by looking for the glorious appearing of the Lord Jesus Christ. "Beloved, now are we the sons [children] of God, and it doth not yet appear what we shall be: but we know that, when he shall appear, we shall be like him; for we shall see him as he is. And every man that hath this hope in him purifieth himself, even as he is pure" (John 3:2, 3). There is a striking certainty in the words "we know that, when he shall appear, we shall be like him; for we shall see him as he is." Here is no "if" nor any condition of human conduct or merit. It is something that every child of God, however weak or failing, may look forward to with full assurance. This is so, only because it is a provision of God's infinite grace. On this fact, that every child of God shall be conformed to the image of His Son, is based the admonition, "Every man that hath this hope in him purifieth himself."

Grace teaches to look for His appearing with a full assurance of having part in it, and then says, let that certain hope influence your life here on earth. Grace says, You shall become like the Son of God; in anticipation thereof, live a life as pure as is He into whose image you shall be transformed.

No man-made religion has ever offered such an appeal to its followers. The appeals of these are always offers of reward for human merit. It is significant that whenever there has been any corruption of true Christianity, this method used by grace to teach purity of life, and godly living, is immediately lost. In the place of the teachings of grace are substituted appeals based on human merit and on fear.

Some teach that unless one measures up to certain standards (never clearly defined) he shall not be received up with Christ when He returns for His own. This makes purity of living a condition for being changed into the image of the Son of God and is a contradiction of the clear teaching by grace.

If being transformed into the likeness of the Lord Jesus Christ and entering into a glorious eternity with Him should in the least degree depend upon living up to certain standards, such living would be for personal gain. The motive then would be selfish, and that life would not be lived entirely unto God. Only when God, as under grace, freely gives everything, apart from any and all human merit, is a life entirely for God made possible.

It should not pass unnoticed that the standard of purity which this appeal calls for is nothing less than the purity of the Son of God. It seems pertinent to ask, Do those who teach the need of a pure life as a condition for being received by the Lord at His return set this same high standard? They do not. In fact, they dare not; for by that standard none would be taken. Their standards must necessarily be possible of general attainment. That is not all, those standards are indefinite and vary for different groups and generations. The appeal becomes one for a purity according to limited and variable human standards and not according to God's absolute standard, the purity of His own Son. All appeals for purity of life as a condition for being received by the Lord are not only contrary to God's appeal, but call for a "godliness" according to human standards, that is not worthy of God.

The climax to Paul's great treatise on the resurrection of believers, which shall take place at the appearing of the Lord Jesus Christ, is in part as follows: "Behold, I shew you a mystery; We shall not all sleep, but we shall all be changed, In a moment, in the twinkling of an eye, at the last trump: for the trumpet shall sound, and the dead shall be raised incorruptible, and we shall be changed. For this corruptible must put on incorruption, and this mortal, must put on immortality." Then death shall be swallowed up in victory (1 Cor. 15:51–54). Herein is a strong note of certainty and assurance for every believer as to the future state. On this is based an appeal for a stable life filled with good works for the Lord. "Therefore, my beloved brethren, be ye steadfast, unmovable, always abounding in the work of the Lord, forasmuch as ye know that your labour is not in vain in the Lord" (v. 58).

Grace then in teaching believers to look for the appearing of the great God and Saviour, Jesus Christ, points to the fact that they are His children; that the Lord Jesus Christ shall return and receive them unto himself, and that all shall be conformed to His image. Furthermore, grace teaches that these things may now be known. These certain facts become the unanswerable arguments for an untroubled heart and a pure life abounding in labor in the Lord.

To teach believers that they are born again and now have eternal life, to constantly remind of the imminent return of the Lord and the glory that shall follow, and to show that all of this springs from the grace of God; is the God-given method to prompt believers to a pure and holy life, a life free from a troubled heart and filled with good works. To omit these truths, and apart from them urge Christians to so live, is to make an appeal on merely human grounds.